Praise for
Win the Day

"Those who have never run a marathon might find it surprising that the scariest place to be when running a marathon isn't the dreaded 'wall' at mile twenty; it's the starting line. Why? Because the runner is overwhelmed by the difficulty and scope of the road ahead and has lost touch with the present moment. In *Win the Day,* Mark equips you to tackle your long-term goals by winning the moment in front of you. I've found this principle to be of paramount importance not only to my athletic success but also to my successful day-to-day living. I am so grateful that Mark wrote this book, and I know it will unlock readers' full potential."

—RYAN HALL, two-time Olympian and fastest American
to ever run the marathon and half marathon

"This book will change the trajectory of your life and help you lead at a higher level. No matter what arena you work in, these daily habits based on timeless principles will help you stress less and accomplish more. I've been personally impacted by Mark's writing, and I know you will be too."

—JOHN MAXWELL, #1 *New York Times* bestselling author,
entrepreneur, and leadership expert

"The pace of life in the modern world keeps most of us on overdrive. Many productivity books simply add more dos to your to-do list. But not *Win the Day.* Instead of teaching you how to do more, Mark will teach you how to win more at what you do."

—JENNI CATRON, leadership coach and founder
of the 4Sight Group

"In this intensely practical book, Mark helps us see that *someday* starts *today.* He gives us simple daily habits that help us form our future. Looking for a better tomorrow? You have to start today. This book will show you how to stop hesitating, stay focused, and change your story for good."

—TIM SCOTT, U.S. Senator

"The easy path may be more convenient, but it's never as fulfilling. Instead of looking backward at what could have been, start looking forward at what could be! Mark Batterson's *Win the Day* will help you step away from the familiar and onto the path of accomplishing your God-sized dreams."

—CRAIG GROESCHEL, pastor of Life.Church
and *New York Times* bestselling author

"At a time when life seems more overwhelming than ever, Mark Batterson offers seven practical habits that can help you overcome your regrets and accomplish what you're called to do every day. Mark's characteristic research, insight, and optimism make *Win the Day* a powerful combination of inspiration and application. The best way to change your life is to start by changing today. This book will help you do just that."

—CAREY NIEUWHOF, bestselling author,
podcast host, and speaker

"*Win the Day* is a timely guide to stressing less in a world that gives us more than enough to stress about. Mark Batterson gives you seven practical steps for living boldly, accomplishing more, and seizing hold of God-sized dreams."

—RYAN SAUNDERS, head coach of the Minnesota Timberwolves

"Sometimes we worry about the future so much that we fail to make the most of right now. It's a trap we can all fall into (and it's so common that we don't even realize we're stuck). In *Win the Day,* Mark gives practical handles to help you accomplish God-sized dreams—one day at a time."

—STEVEN FURTICK, pastor of Elevation Church
and *New York Times* bestselling author

Win the Day

Win the Day

7 Daily Habits to Help You

Stress Less & Accomplish More

MARK BATTERSON

MULTNOMAH

To my grandparents Elmer and Alene Johnson.
Your legacy of faith bears fruit to the third and
fourth generations—and beyond.

Contents

Introduction

Day-Tight Compartments

Almost anybody can accomplish almost anything
if they work at it long enough, hard enough,
and smart enough.

In 1871, a twenty-one-year-old medical student read one sentence that would change the trajectory of his life. At the time, the pressure of final exams and the prospect of starting a medical practice led to a near nervous breakdown. William Osler was destined to become the most famous medical doctor of his generation. He would organize the Johns Hopkins School of Medicine, establish the first residency program for specialty training, and write the predominant medical textbook of his era.[1]

The Father of Modern Medicine would even be knighted Sir William by the king of England. Of course, Osler knew none of this at twenty-one. None of us do. All he knew was that he was overwhelmed by what felt like the weight of the world. That's when twenty-two words, written by the Scottish historian Thomas Carlyle, changed everything: "Our grand business undoubtedly is, not to *see* what lies dimly at a distance, but to *do* what lies clearly at hand."[2]

Forty-two years later, Sir William Osler delivered an address at Yale University on April 20, 1913.[3] Despite his distinguished credentials, Osler professed intellectual averageness. His success was not the by-product of innate intelligence or natural talent. What, then, could explain his success? Osler traced it back to the twenty-two words that had altered his outlook on life. He took those words—"*Do* what lies clearly at hand"—and put his fingerprints on them. Reflecting on his own insecurities and uncertainties, Osler issued a timeless challenge to those students:

Live in day-tight compartments.[4]

"The load of to-morrow," said Osler, "added to that of yesterday, carried to-day makes the strongest falter."[5] It's true, isn't it? We feel overwhelmed by yesterday's mistakes and underqualified for tomorrow's opportunities. We feel so overwhelmed, so underqualified, that we're tempted to quit before we even start. And that's what many people do. Their lives are over before they even begin. They stop living and start dying.

More than a century later, Osler's words still echo. In a day of endless distractions, an age of ceaseless change, they ring true now more than ever. So many people are so overwhelmed by so many things! We're paralyzed by things we *cannot change*—the past. We're crippled by things we *cannot control*—the future. The solution? Osler's age-old advice is as good a place to start as any: let go of "dead yesterdays" and "unborn to-morrows."[6]

The secret to Sir William Osler's success is the solution to a thousand problems. Instead of fixating on things that lie dimly at a distance, concentrate on what lies clearly at hand. Simply put, focus on inputs rather than outcomes. If yesterday is history and tomorrow is mystery, win the day! When you win today, tomorrow takes care of itself. Do that enough days in a row and you can accomplish almost anything!

How do you win the day? For starters, you have to define the win: *What's important now?* Identify the lead measures that will produce the results you want. Establish daily rituals that will make your life more meaningful. Break bad habits by establishing good habits; then habit stack those high-yield habits in a way that will pay dividends down the road. In the pages that follow, I'll unpack all these ideas and many more.

A few months before delivering his day-tight address, William Osler had crossed the Atlantic on an ocean liner. While standing on the bridge of that ship, he had an aha moment. The captain was demonstrating the latest and greatest in maritime technology. He pressed a button that shifted gears, turning parts of that ship into watertight compartments.

Leveraging that machinery as a metaphor, Osler likened each of us to an ocean liner on a long voyage. "What I urge is that you so learn to control the machinery as to live with 'day-tight compartments,'" he said. "Touch a button and hear, at every level of your life, the iron doors shutting out the Past—the dead yesterdays. Touch another and shut off, with a metal curtain, the Future—the unborn to-morrows."[7]

This book is all about pressing that button and unleashing the power of twenty-four hours. Burying dead yesterdays can be as difficult as a graveside funeral. Imagining unborn tomorrows involves no less labor than childbirth. But if you want to win the day, there is no other way.

Fully Alive

While teaching at the University of Pennsylvania, Dr. Tony Campolo once turned an ordinary lecture into an unforgettable lesson. He asked an unsuspecting student sitting in the front row, "Young man, how long have you lived?" The student answered his age. Tony responded, "No, no, no. That's how long your heart has been pumping blood. That's not how long you have lived."

Tony Campolo then told the class about one of the most memorable moments of his life. In 1944, his fourth-grade class took a field trip to the top of the Empire State Building. It was the tallest building in the world at the time. When nine-year-old Tony got off the elevator and stepped onto the observation deck overlooking New York City, time stood still. "In one mystical, magical moment I took in the city," he said. "If I live a million years, that moment will still be part of my consciousness, because I was fully alive when I lived it."

Tony turned back to the student. "Now, let me ask you the question again. How long have you lived?" The student sheepishly said, "When you say it that way, maybe an hour; maybe a minute; maybe two minutes."[8]

How long have you lived? I mean *really* lived. It's easy calculating age. It's more difficult quantifying life. Why? Because *time is measured in minutes, while life is measured in moments.* What are those top-of-the-Empire-State-Building moments for you? For most of us, they are too few and far between. When was the last time that time stood still? And if you turned those moments into minutes, how long have you lived?

According to psychologists Matthew Killingsworth and Daniel Gilbert, the average person spends 46.9 percent of their time thinking about something other than what they're doing in the present moment.[9] We're half-present half the time, which means we're half-alive.

The only way to be fully alive is to be fully present, and the only way to be fully present is to live in day-tight compartments. For far too many of us, life feels like the meaningless passage of time between far too few meaningful moments. And even when they do come along, we take selfies instead of being fully present. We miss the moment because we're living in the wrong time zone. We're so fixated on the past and so anxious about the future that we miss the present. Then we wonder where life went.

The future is right here, right now—the eternal now. Heaven is invading earth. Eternity is invading time. Most people falsely assume that eternity starts at some point in the far-off future, and they live accordingly. Eternity is counterclockwise. Eternity is invading time every second of every minute of every hour of every day!

"Every now is an eternity," said Frank Laubach, "if it is full of God."[10]

COUNT THE DAYS

Long before digital clocks and calendars, an ancient poet said, "Teach us to number our days, that we may gain a heart of wisdom."[11] If you want every day to count, you have to count the days. How? Try counting backward.

This may seem a little sadistic, but if you're the curious type, pay a visit to deathclock.com. Go ahead—this book will still be here when you get back. Enter your birthday, along with your body-mass index, and it spits out your estimated day of death. My favorite feature? You can choose between normal, sadistic, pessimistic, and optimistic settings! The optimistic setting gets me to age ninety-three, which falls short of my goal of living to one hundred. Of course, there isn't an option for *eternal* optimists!

What does it mean to win the day? It's living like each day is the first day and last day of your life, which is both an art and a science. I'll tell stories, cite studies, and share best practices. Together, we'll build seven habits designed to help you *win the day*. This process won't be easy, and it won't happen overnight. But if you put these seven habits into practice, you'll win a lot more days than you lose! You'll learn how to stress less and accomplish more.

In part 1, we'll *bury dead yesterdays*. Memory is both a blessing and a curse. Without it, we'd have to relearn everything every day! The challenge, of course, is remembering right. We have a tendency to remember what we should forget and forget what we should remember. That's how we get stuck in a moment. If you want God to do something new, you can't keep doing the same old thing. The first two habits—*flip the script* and *kiss the wave*—will help you rewrite your narrative and process your pain. If you feel like a prisoner of your past, prepare to be set free!

In part 2, we'll turn the page on the past and *win the day*. Tomorrow may be a mystery, but destiny is not! Destiny is a daily decision. Over time, those daily decisions yield compound interest. If you do the right things day in and day out, God is going to show up and show off. I can't tell you when or where or how. And it'll be on His terms, His timeline! But I do know this: you cannot break the law of sowing and reaping. It will make or break you. The good news? You are only one decision away from a totally different life! The next two habits—*eat the frog* and *fly the kite*—will help you make the right predecisions and establish the right rituals.

In part 3, we'll flip to the future and *imagine unborn tomorrows.* Show me the size of your dream, and I'll show you the size of your God. The ability to imagine the future is a function of your right brain and is one dimension of the image of God. If you're going to dream big, you've got to think long. The next two habits—*cut the rope* and *wind the clock*—will help you take the right risks and play the long game a little better.

Finally, we'll *seed the clouds* with the seventh habit. The only moment we ever have is *now*—it's now or never! You've got to *learn* like you'll live forever, but you've got to *live* like there's no tomorrow. You are here for such a time as this. You are here for such a place as this. It's time to live that way.

Can I make two recommendations as you board this ocean liner, press the button that shifts your life into day-tight compartments, and embark on this journey?

First, take it one habit at a time. If you try to make too many changes at the same time, the chance of success goes way down. Don't get overwhelmed. Pick a habit—any habit—and go to work on it. Rome wasn't built in a day, right? It'll take consistent effort over weeks and months and years to win the day. I hope this book feels like an old friend that you turn to often.

Second, I'd recommend reading this book with a friend, with a team, or with your staff. You'll certainly benefit if you read it by yourself, but there is synergy when a book is read in community. While holding you accountable, a community gives you a built-in sounding board.

THE TWENTY-FOUR-HOUR RULE

A few years ago, I had the privilege of meeting NFL Hall of Famer Emmitt Smith. Emmitt holds the NFL record for all-time rushing yards—18,355. That adds up to 10.4 miles on the odometer, and that's with three-hundred-pound defensive tackles giving him a flat tire every 4.2 yards! How did Emmitt do it? One game at a time, one play at a time, one yard at a time!

During a panel session we cochaired, Emmitt shared one secret to his success. He called it "the twenty-four-hour rule." Win or lose, Emmitt gave himself a twenty-four-hour window to celebrate the win or lament the loss. Sounds a lot like Osler's day-tight compartments, doesn't it? The next day, it was back to business, back to basics. "It never ends," said Emmitt. "If you play the game to win one Super Bowl or two Super Bowls and then be satisfied, you are playing for the wrong reason. No matter how much you win, you want to win more."[12]

What if we applied the twenty-four-hour rule to all of life?

I bet we'd gain a lot more yardage and win a lot more days!

I love Emmitt Smith's unique application, but the twenty-four-hour rule is nothing new. It's the centerpiece of the most famous prayer of all time: "Give us this day our daily bread."[13] Even those who aren't religious recognize it, perhaps have even prayed it. In his address, William Osler challenged the Yale students to pray that piece of the Lord's Prayer every day.[14] As the son of a pastor, Osler knew it well. He also knew that praying it every day was much easier said than done!

Can I tell you what I wish it said? "Give us this *week* our *weekly* bread." Better yet, "Give us this *year* our *yearly* bread." That would be so much easier, wouldn't it? That way, we wouldn't have to depend on God every day. But that, of course, is the point of the prayer. That is its genius.

The Lord's Prayer is three-dimensional—it helps us nullify past mistakes, navigate present circumstances, and negotiate future challenges. Jesus prayed past tense: "Forgive us our debts, as we also have forgiven our debtors."[15] You cannot change the past, but you can leverage its lessons. Then you've got to pull a *Frozen* and let it go. Jesus prayed future tense: "Lead us not into temptation."[16] You cannot control the future, but you can make predecisions today that will pay dividends tomorrow.

Finally, Jesus prayed present tense: "Give us this day our daily bread."[17] We want God to provide *more* so we can trust Him *less,* but He loves us too much to do that. God will never give us more than we can steward, which is one reason time is divided into days. All we have to do is live in the way He intended—in day-tight compartments.

Do you remember the expiration date on manna? *One day.*[18] How about the deadline on anger? *Sundown.*[19] When are God's mercies made new? *Every morning.*[20] How often are we told to take up our crosses? *Daily.*[21] And when are we told to rejoice and be glad? *Today!*[22] The twenty-four-hour rule is everywhere you look! In fact, it's as old as day one.

There was evening and there was morning, the first day.[23]

It's not insignificant, by the way, that the first day begins with sundown! We'll rediscover that ancient rhythm when we explore daily rituals, but let's not get ahead of ourselves.

Do It for a Day

Remember Tony Campolo's unforgettable moment atop the Empire State Building? If I live a million years, rafting the Colorado River through the Grand Canyon with a handful of friends will be part of my consciousness forever. The trip doubled as a rite of passage for my younger son, Josiah. We were up at the crack of dawn every morning, trying to beat the heat. Temperatures topped out around 108 degrees every day. Fortunately, the water temperature was roughly half the air temperature, so we cooled off in a New York minute. For five unforgettable days, we rafted rapids, hiked side canyons, and slept under the stars.

When you spend every waking hour on a raft, on a trail, or around a campsite, you have time to talk. During one of those fireside chats, Matthew Barnett asked a question that revolutionized the way I live and the way I lead. For me, it's on par with the twenty-two words written by Thomas Carlyle and read by William Osler.

Matthew is a friend and cofounder of the LA Dream Center, which has helped tens of thousands of people who find themselves at the end of their ropes. Many of them are trying to overcome life-controlling addictions or rebuild broken lives. No matter what habits they're trying to break or what goals they're going after, Matthew asks them this question:

Can you do it for a day?

There is a simple kind of genius to that question. Why do so many problems remain unresolved? Why do so many bad habits remain unbroken? Why do so many goals remain unachieved? Nine times out of ten, we're so overwhelmed by the size of the problem or the habit or the goal that we give up before we even get started.

Since Matthew introduced me to that question, I've asked it of lots of people facing lots of challenges. No one has ever said no. Not one! Why? Because anyone can do anything for a day! Do you think you can do it for a week? *Probably.* Or a month? *Maybe.* Or a year? *I'm not so sure.* As the timeline gets longer, so do the odds. How about the rest of your life? I won't even answer that one. Can you do it for a day? *Now, that I can do!* The odds of success get greater as the time compartments get smaller. If you get it down to day-tight compartments, anything is possible!

By the end of January, 75 percent of people fail to keep their New Year's resolutions.[24] Why? When you think in one-year time frames, the finish is so far away you can't even see it. We'd gain a lot more ground if we focused on habits rather than goals and did so one day at a time.

I have no idea what problem you're trying to solve, what habit you're trying to break or build, or what God-sized goal you're going after. I'm not sure how you define the win, but I know the secret to your success. It was the same for William Osler and Emmitt Smith. You've got to win the day in front of you! Do so two days in a row, and you've got a winning streak!

Before turning the page, identify a habit—any habit. Set a goal, any goal. Got it? Now let me ask a question. You know what's coming, don't you?

Can you do it for a day?

You know you can! All you have to do is live in day-tight compartments. It's time to unleash the power of twenty-four hours.

PART ONE

Bury Dead Yesterdays

From 1837 until 1901, Queen Victoria ruled the British Empire. Her sixty-three-year reign set the record in Britain, only to be broken by her great-great-granddaughter Queen Elizabeth II. Victoria's name came to define an era, the Victorian age.

Not long after assuming the throne, Queen Victoria fell in love with Francis Albert Augustus Charles Emmanuel. She proposed to him five days after his arrival at Windsor Castle, and they were married on February 10, 1840. The following is her diary entry about her wedding day:

> *I NEVER, NEVER spent such an evening!! My DEAR-*
> *EST DEAREST DEAR Albert . . . his excessive love and*
> *affection gave me feelings of heavenly love and happiness I*
> *never could have hoped to have felt before! He clasped me*
> *in his arms, and we kissed each other again and again! His*
> *beauty, his sweetness and gentleness—really how can I*
> *ever be thankful enough to have such a Husband! . . . to be*
> *called by names of tenderness, I have never yet heard used*
> *to me before—was bliss beyond belief! Oh! this was the*
> *happiest day of my life![1]*

Talk about the top of the Empire State Building! I think it's safe to say that Queen Victoria won the day on her wedding day. In fact, it sounds like she won the dating lottery! Nine months later, she gave birth to her namesake, Princess Victoria.

The Queen wasn't fond of pregnancy, and she apparently thought that newborn babies were ugly. Nevertheless, she and Prince Albert had—count them—nine children. I'm guessing that dear Albert's "excessive love and affection" had something to do with that.

The royal couple had been married twenty-one years when Prince Albert contracted typhoid fever and died. Victoria entered a period of profound grief from which she would never recover. She had Albert's room turned into a shrine. Every day for the rest of her life, she had the linens on Albert's bed changed, his clothes laid out, and a basin of water poured for his morning shave. She even slept with Albert's nightshirt in her arms.[2]

When we experience loss, a piece of us dies with the person that passes. But Queen Victoria stopped living altogether. The Widow of Windsor rarely left the palace and wore only black the rest of her life. Queen Victoria died on January 22, 1901, but she stopped living the day Albert died—December 14, 1861. I did the math. That adds up to 14,283 days!

I wish Queen Victoria were the exception to the rule, but you and I know she's not. Most people stop living long before they breathe their last. Why? They become prisoners of their past—past mistakes, past hurts, past offenses. If you live long enough, you will experience profound pain and suffering. There is no escaping this reality. Life is unfair; then you die. I know—slightly depressing. The good news? You can bury those hurts and habits and hang-ups. A new day is gonna dawn! "A change is gonna come!"[3]

To be fair, we live in a culture that isn't good at grief. Because we're uncomfortable with it, we often move on too quickly, too easily. You've got to own the pain so the pain doesn't own you. You've got to look it square in the eye and learn its lessons.

There is a genius to the Jewish way of grieving, allotting a predetermined number of days to different types of mourning. When Job was mourning the loss of his children, his friends sat with him in silence for seven days.[4] That weeklong mourning period for first-degree relatives is a Jewish ritual called sitting shiva. This is where we've got to give people an extra measure of grace. We give them elbow room, breathing room. You never get over the loss of a loved one. This I know from personal experience. But with God's help, you can get through it and get on with the business of living.

Queen Victoria owed it to her empire to keep living, to keep leading. She owed it to her children. She owed it to Albert. She owed it to herself. When we fail to bury dead yesterdays, we aren't doing a disservice just to ourselves. We're cheating everyone we love, including God. Go ahead and give your dead yesterdays a eulogy. But once you do, let them rest in peace. In this book, there are seven habits dedicated to helping you stress less and accomplish more. The first two habits—*flip the script* and *kiss the wave*—focus on the past. You aren't ready to win the day until you bury dead yesterdays six feet deep.

Habit 1—Flip the Script

If you want to change your life,
start by changing your story.

In 1934, the pastor of Ebenezer Baptist Church in Atlanta sailed across the Atlantic Ocean on his maiden voyage to the Holy Land. I'm not sure whether it was the same ship William Osler sailed on, but that trip changed his trajectory. On his return trip, Michael King attended a gathering of the Baptist World Alliance in Berlin. While there, he became captivated by the Protestant Reformer Martin Luther. Luther's protestations against the religious establishment of his day inspired King's own convictions related to the civil rights movement. Luther's brave became King's breakthrough!

To honor Luther's legacy, Michael King changed his name to Martin Luther King. He had a five-year-old son, his namesake. Not long after changing his own name, Michael-turned-Martin renamed his son as well. For the rest of his son's life, close relatives still called him Mike. The rest of the world knew him as Dr. Martin Luther King Jr.[1]

In 1964, a boxer named Cassius Clay began a new chapter of his life with a new name, Muhammad Ali. In 1993, the artist formerly known as Prince changed his stage name to a symbol. The composer Johannes Chrysostomus Wolfgangus Theophilus Mozart altered his name multiple times. Why? It's not just because it was way too long. According to one biographer, "Mozart's constant alterations of his name are his way of experimenting with different identities."[2] You'd be surprised—or maybe not—how many of Hollywood's household names are nicknames. Vin Diesel is way too cool to be a birth name, right? You are correct. The same is true of Joaquin Phoenix, Jamie Foxx, and Whoopi Goldberg. You can add Elton John, John Legend, and Lady Gaga to the mix.

I have a habit of nicknaming just about everybody I know. The more I love someone, the more nicknames I give that person. It's amazing our kids even know their birth names, because I gave them so many nicknames! What can I say? There aren't enough names to capture the dimensions of my love for them. I'd like to think that I'm following in the heavenly Father's footsteps. God turned Abram into Abraham and Sarai into Sarah. The switch from Jacob to Israel was more than just a name change—it was a new story, a new identity, a new destiny, a new nation. And the apple didn't fall far from the Father's tree. Jesus gave nicknames to everyone! My favorite? He called His cousins James and John "sons of thunder"![3]

Did you know that God has a unique name for you? The name your parents gave you when you were born is a placeholder. Your real name won't be revealed until the day you die: "I will give him a white stone, with a new name written on the stone that no one knows except the one who receives it."[4]

What does any of that have to do with winning the day? Or burying dead yesterdays? The difference between success and failure is the stories we tell ourselves. True or false, those stories become self-fulfilling prophecies. If you tell yourself the wrong story, you live a lie. If you want to change your life, start by changing your story.

Why does God give us a new name? It's His way of flipping the script. And it's not any old name. It's actually *His* name. There is an ancient blessing you've probably heard a time or two:

> The LORD bless you
> and keep you;

the LORD make his face shine on you
>   and be gracious to you;
the LORD turn his face toward you
>   and give you peace.

We usually stop right there, but that's not even the best part. It's the postscript that packs the punch: "So they will put my name on the Israelites, and I will bless them."[5]

God doesn't just rename us; He puts *His* name on us. There are more than four hundred names for God in Scripture. Which one does He put on us? All of them! This is how God flips the script. He changes our name, which changes our identity. We get grafted into God's story. God writes His-story—*history* with a hyphen—through us.

If your life isn't what you want it to be, it may be because you're telling yourself the wrong story! Your *explanations* are more important than your *experiences*. Your *stories* are more important than the *situations* you find yourself in.

It's time to flip the script.

1

Signature Story

Live your life in a way that is worth telling stories about.

On August 22, 1851, Commodore John Cox Stevens and his six-man crew won the America's Cup in a fifty-three-mile regatta around the Isle of Wight. The race was witnessed by Queen Victoria, who reportedly asked which yacht was second. The infamous answer? "Ah, Your Majesty, there is no second."[1] Thus began one of the most impressive winning streaks in history.

The New York Yacht Club, of which Commodore Stevens was a founding member, successfully defended the cup for 132 years. They were undefeated until September 26, 1983, when the *Australia II*, skippered by John Bertrand, ended the longest winning streak in sporting history with a forty-one-second margin of victory.[2]

That win was a milestone moment for Australia, hailed like a national holiday. Even America tipped its cap to the *Australia II*. It was awarded Athlete of the Year by ABC's *Wide World of Sports*. I'm not sure how a *boat* wins that award, but that's water under the bridge. The question is this: How was the *Australia II* able to do what no one had done in 132 years? A winged keel designed by Dutch engineers certainly gave the Australian team a technical advantage, but that isn't what won the race.

If you haven't tasted victory in 132 years, it's hard to imagine any outcome other than defeat. The first thing you need to do is convince yourself that winning is possible. How? The answer is the first habit—*flip the script*. You've got to rewrite your narrative by telling yourself a different story, a better story.

Several years before the 1983 America's Cup, the Australian skipper, Mike Fletcher, had read the classic novella *Jonathan Livingston Seagull*. The moral of that story? "Begin by knowing that you have already arrived."[3] Sounds like Stephen Covey's second habit of highly effective people: "Begin with the end in mind."[4] Inspired by *Seagull's* story line, Fletcher made a recording of the Australian team winning the race. The recording included narration and the sound of a sailboat cutting through the water. A copy of that recording was given to each member of the crew, and they were instructed to listen to it twice a day. They did this—get this—*every day* for three years! Before even setting sail, they had won the race 2,190 times![5]

How did the Australian team bury a long losing streak? They flipped the flipping script! They told themselves a different story over and over again. They won the race because they won the day—1,095 days in a row!

According to cybernetic theory, there are two types of change. First-order change is *behavioral*—it's doing things more or less. If you're trying to lose weight, eating less and exercising more is a step in the right direction. First-order change is effective as a quick fix, but second-order change passes the test of time. Second-order change is *conceptual*—it's mind over matter. It's rewriting the narrative.

Change your story; change your life!

RUNT OF THE LITTER

When Bo Eason was nine years old, he drew a self-portrait on a piece of paper. I've seen the sketch up close and personal. The stick figure isn't impressive, artistically speaking. The caption beneath it is what caught my eye: "the best safety in the NFL."

That is the goal Bo set for himself at the age of nine. There was one small problem with that Goliath-sized goal, and I mean that literally. At Bo's first practice with his high school football team, every player was measured and weighed. Bo was found wanting. He measured five feet tall and weighed one hundred pounds. Based on the coach's expression, Bo Eason had no business playing football.

After practice, Bo said to his dad, "The coach thinks I'm too small to play." Without skipping a beat, Bo's dad said, "Did they measure your heart?" All I want is one moment like that as a father! Talk about nailing the landing, but it gets even better. Bo's dad then told him a story that would flip his script and alter his identity.

Nothing is more valuable to a rancher than his ranch dog. As a former ranch hand, Bo's father would know. The ranch dog does the work of ten men, herding the cattle and getting them where the rancher wants them to go. When a ranch dog has puppies, the rancher identifies the smallest puppy—the runt of the litter—by tying a piece of yarn around its neck. After twelve weeks, the rancher gives away all the puppies except for the runt of the litter. Why? As Bo's dad said, "The runt always has to work harder to survive against its bigger brothers and sisters. Always. The runt becomes the smartest, the fastest, the most determined. Of all the puppies, the runt's heart is the biggest. The rancher stakes his whole livelihood on that fact."[6]

As the youngest of six kids, Bo took his father's message to heart. He would have to work harder, work smarter, and work longer than everybody else! That's when Bo made a contract with himself, vowing to be the first player on the practice field and the last player off it every day. Bo Eason kept that contract for twenty years!

AGAINST THE ODDS

The odds of playing in the NFL are astronomical. More than a million kids play high school football, but there are only thirty-two NFL teams with fifty-three-man rosters. That totals 1,696 spots for a million hopefuls! The odds are 1 in 589, less than 0.2 percent. I can almost guarantee that just about everyone who makes an NFL roster weighed more than a hundred pounds in high school, but I bet very few of them have a bigger heart or a better story than Bo.

Bo Eason was the first safety chosen in the 1984 NFL draft, earning All-Pro honors his second season with the Houston Oilers. Remember the contract he made with himself to be the first player on and the last player off the practice field? He kept that contract until he was traded to the San Francisco 49ers. On the first day of training camp, Bo got dressed an hour and a half before practice started. But when he got onto the practice field, Jerry Rice was already there. Of course, coming in second to arguably the greatest receiver in NFL history isn't half-bad.

How did Bo Eason beat the odds? He defined the win: *What's important now?* Then he painted a picture of his preferred future. That's what faith looks like—it's being sure of what we hope for and certain of what we do not see.[7] But setting a God-sized goal wasn't enough. The defining moment was the day his dad flipped the script with a story. Bo Eason owned that story; then that story owned him. It became his signature story—the story that changed his identity and defined his destiny.

"I made that dog's story my story," Bo said. "And I've been telling myself that story ever since."[8] Bo Eason flipped the script on the high school coach who didn't think he was football material. After a knee injury ended his NFL career, Bo flipped the script a second time by turning his signature story into a Broadway play, *Runt of the Litter.*

What stories are you telling yourself? And where do they come from? Are they helping you or hurting you? Are they accurate or inaccurate? Are they carefully crafted or off the cuff? And who is narrating the story? You? Your parents? Your doubters? Your haters? Or have you given editorial control to the Author and Perfecter of your faith?[9]

"Every person is composed of a few themes," observed C. S. Lewis.[10] Those *life themes* reveal themselves in a wide variety of ways. Sometimes it's during the regular routine of life. More often than not, it's something out of the ordinary. One way or the other, something happens that strikes a chord at the core of your being. A God-sized dream or God-ordained passion is conceived deep within your spirit. It's the thing that gets you up early and keeps you up late. It's the thing that makes you smile, makes you cry, or makes you pound your fist on the table. Those life themes become the subplots of your life, and they undergird everything you do.

SUBPLOTS

A few years ago, I spent two days with a life coach doing a life plan.[11] It consisted of eighteen exercises, some of which I'll share. The first exercise was archaeological, digging into my past. Why? Your destiny is hidden in your history. Lots of clues and cues that can help you win the day.

Everything in your past is preparation for something in your future! God doesn't waste days, especially bad days! My life coach helped me identify forty-four defining moments. Some were as dramatic as the day I almost died from ruptured intestines. I was surprised, however, at how many defining moments were as subtle as the subconscious. Identifying those subplots is one key to flipping the script, so I'll share a few of mine.

When I was kid, I was playing Kick the Can with my friends when my mom rang the dinner bell. That's how we texted before cell phones! We sat down at the dinner table, and I remember saying, "We've got to hurry up and eat because my friends are waiting." I wasn't having a panic attack, but my sense of urgency was acute. We couldn't eat fast enough! Why? I didn't want to keep my friends waiting. I wish it were nothing more than five-year-old FOMO—fear of missing out.

I know that incident sounds totally insignificant. Truth be told? It's the story of my life. Even at five, I felt tremendous internal tension at the thought of letting others down. If there is a twelve-step program for people pleasers, sign me up. I recently shared that subplot with my counselor, including this confession: "I don't want to disappoint anyone ever." My counselor said, "That's an awfully big burden to bear." Yes, it is! Then he added this: "You know, Mark, Jesus disappointed just about everyone." Ouch. Trying to please everyone all the time is *not* the Jesus way. Quite the opposite. If you follow Jesus, you'll offend more than a few pharisees along the way.

Let me share one more subplot, with the goal of helping you identify yours. Around the same time as the inciting incident I just shared, a neighbor-friend knocked on my door and announced that I could no longer ride his banana-seat bike. Why? Because his dad had removed the training wheels. Do not—I repeat, do not—tell me what I cannot do! I marched myself down to his house, got on his bike, and rode it back to my house minus the training wheels! I'll never forget the feeling of kicking down that kickstand in my driveway, having done something that my neighbor didn't think I could do. It's another one of those *top-of-the-Empire-State-Building* or *bottom-of-the-Grand-Canyon* moments.

If you want me to do something, don't tell me what to do. That's totally demotivating. Tell me it can't be done! *You can't wash the dishes in five minutes. You can't remember to take out the garbage. You can't fix the toilet.* I wish I were kidding! Lora has to live with this personality trait, but she has learned my love language! For better or for worse, I love proving people wrong. Especially the so-called experts! It's not only the way I'm wired; it undergirds this entire book.

I Have a Hypothesis

I have a hypothesis. I know, not nearly as notable as Dr. King's "I Have a Dream." All right, my hypothesis doubles as my dream: *almost anybody can accomplish almost anything if they work at it long enough, hard enough, and smart enough.*

You are capable of more than you imagine, and I wrote this book to help you prove it to yourself. Your brain has no idea what your body is capable of, and your body has no idea what your brain is capable of.

Once you connect those dots, all bets are off. Following Jesus is less about minding your p's and q's than it is about taking your cues from Christ. What did Jesus say? "With God all things are possible."[12] When you give complete editorial control of your life to Him, *possible* becomes the plotline.

I'd better offer one disclaimer to my hypothesis. Please note the word *almost*. If you're five foot seven, genetic factors call into question your dream of playing in the NBA. Be that as it may, may I remind you that Spud Webb won the NBA dunk contest in 1986. *Don't tell me it can't be done!* It has been done, and it will be done again. I won't ignore the genetic and epigenetic challenges many of us have to overcome, and I'll tell you why. Because, contrary to popular opinion, we don't succeed *in spite of* those disadvantages, difficulties, or disappointments. We succeed *because of* them, if we learn how to leverage them. So, once again for good measure:

> Almost anybody can accomplish almost anything if they work
> at it long enough, hard enough, and smart enough.

Yes, you. Not only do I believe it; I'm also evidence of it. I've written books that have sold millions of copies, but according to an aptitude assessment in graduate school, writing is *not* a natural gifting. "Whatever you do, don't write books!" Of course, all I needed was that dare! In retrospect, I'm grateful that writing didn't come naturally. Why? I had to work longer, work harder, and work smarter. If I was going to be a writer, I knew I had to become a reader. So I read three thousand books before I wrote one.

Guess where I discovered the idea of living in day-tight compartments? In a 1944 book written by Dale Carnegie: *How to Stop Worrying and Start Living.* I had no idea at the time, but I was researching *this book* as I read *that book* twenty years ago.

If you have a book in you, I want to help you write it. How? One sentence, one paragraph, one chapter at a time. You can't write a book

in a day! Well, I take that back. In 1945, Aiden Wilson Tozer boarded a
Pullman train at the LaSalle Street Station in Chicago and requested a
writing table. When that train arrived in McAllen, Texas, the next day,
Tozer had a complete draft of an all-time classic, *The Pursuit of God*. If
your name isn't Tozer, it might take a little longer!

Tim Ferriss is the author of several *New York Times* bestsellers, and
they aren't leaflets. His books are thicker than most phone books! How
does Tim do it? "Two crappy pages a day." Tim takes the pressure of
perfectionism off himself by focusing on quantity over quality, which is
brilliant. He sets a goal that is, in his words, "easily winnable."[13]

Ingmar Bergman, director of Academy Award–winning films, said
the same thing in a different way. "Do you know what moviemaking
is?" he asked. "Eight hours of hard work each day to get three minutes
of film."[14] Two crappy pages. Three minutes of film. You can do this, but
you might want to give yourself a daily quota. Don't worry about quality.
Good writing is bad writing well edited. If you write two pages a day,
you'll have a two-hundred-page book in one hundred days. All you have
to do is win the *one* day in front of you, no matter what goal you go after.

MOST LIKELY TO SUCCEED—OR NOT

I was not voted Most Likely to Succeed in junior high or high school. I
was voted Best Dressed, which is unbelievable when I look back at my
yearbook! I consider myself below average at most things. Like William
Osler, I profess intellectual averageness. I have, however, learned how to
leverage my weaknesses. If success is the by-product of well-managed
failure—and I think it is—then strength is the result of well-managed
weakness.

Our subplots reveal both strengths and weaknesses. Signature stories, on the other hand, are almost always born out of crisis, born out of
weakness. An obstacle must be overcome against all odds. It's a story
line that doesn't just make for a good movie; it makes for a good life. It's
the adversities we overcome that make us who we are.

My signature story starts with me waking up in the middle of the night, unable to breathe. My earliest memory is an asthma attack. I was rushed to the emergency room for a shot of epinephrine, and that routine was repeated more times than I care to remember. When asthma is all you can remember, it's hard to imagine anything else. For more than four decades, I suffered from severe asthma. There weren't forty days in forty years that I didn't have to take my rescue inhaler multiple times. I never went anywhere without it—I slept with it under my pillow and played basketball with it in my sock. If you counted all the days I spent in the intensive care unit, they would add up to many months.

Then, on July 2, 2016, I felt prompted to pray a brave prayer. I asked God to heal my asthma, and He miraculously answered. For the record, I had asked God to heal me hundreds of times before. Why He chose to heal me on that particular day, in this particular way, is a mystery to me. But I never lost faith in one simple fact: God is able! Plus, I believe that God honors bold prayers because bold prayers honor God.

There are days, and then there are days that change every day thereafter. The day God healed my asthma is one of those *ever-after* days. A signature story usually centers on a day that begins like any other day; then that day rewrites the rest of your life. I actually keep a running tally, numbering the days I've been inhaler-free.

I have no idea how your story reads right now. I don't know whether it's comedy, drama, or action and adventure. If you don't like your story line, God can change it. He can redeem the loss, recycle the mistake, and rewrite the pain. He can do so in a single day, no doubt. That said, don't wait until your circumstances change to start living your best life!

Despite suffering from severe asthma for forty years, I have biked century rides and run in triathlons. Did I mention my six knee surgeries? Why would I go after those particular goals? Because I love when the odds are stacked against me! If it's easy, what's the point? I want to go after dreams that are destined to fail without divine intervention. I want to accomplish things that I can't take credit for. The harder, the better! God gets more glory! You need some giants in your life. Why? Without Goliath, you don't discover David.

I have one hundred life goals, and you can download them at markbatterson.com/wintheday. You can also download "Seven Steps to Setting Life Goals." I borrowed a few of my goals from others, and you can certainly do the same with mine. But few things will stretch your faith like coming up with your own life goal list. What do those goals have to do with my signature story? Goal setting is storytelling. It's writing the last chapter first, then working your way backward! Your story will be only as good as the goals you go after.

I know that millions of people have run marathons, but running a marathon is something I couldn't even imagine for most of my life because of my severe asthma. That life goal was a late entry. It wasn't until God miraculously healed my asthma that I added it to my life goal list. In 2017, I ran the Chicago Marathon as a way of celebrating God healing my lungs.

To date, I've accomplished about half my life goals. How have I done it? I didn't run that 26.2-mile marathon the day after setting the goal—that's for sure. That's a good way to pull a hamstring. The first thing I did was download a training plan; then I worked the plan. Six months later, I had completed seventy-two training runs totaling 475 miles. That's how you flip the script. It's not by pulling fairy tales out of thin air! It starts by setting a God-sized goal that stretches your faith. Then you go after that goal one mile, one run, one day at a time.

The bigger the goal, the better the story you need to tell yourself. Of course, you can flip that script. The better the story you tell yourself, the bigger the goal you can go after.

TILT THE TREADMILL

Let me add one more subplot to that signature story.

Have you ever heard the name Emil Zátopek? *Runner's World* called him "the greatest runner of all time," yet few people know his name.[15] I picked up a biography on Zátopek the day I started training. His story flipped my script and helped me come in first place. I'm kidding! I did not win the Chicago Marathon—not even close. But I did finish the race, and I never lost my breath, which is even more miraculous to me than winning!

On the day I discovered Emil Zátopek, I went home and announced to my family that I would make a movie about his life if it's the last thing I do. Over the next year, I turned his story into a movie script that I am currently shopping. Yes, making a movie is one of my life goals. Why? Because a film called *The Hiding Place* was a catalyst in my own spiritual journey and I want to flip that blessing. I'm not naive. I know that seeing lots of movies doesn't qualify you to make one! That said, God doesn't call the qualified. He qualifies the called. If it's in God's will and for God's glory, it qualifies for God's favor.

I trained for the Chicago Marathon by myself, but I never ran alone! Emil Zátopek was with me every step of the way. His story became my script, and we crossed that finish line together!

If you choose to go after a God-sized goal, you'd better buckle up. Especially if it doesn't fit within your natural gifting! It's like tilting the treadmill to a steep incline. You'll have to work a little longer, a little harder, and a little smarter than everyone else. It will be harder than you hoped and take longer than you imagined. So be it. If you keep walking in the right direction, you'll get where you're going sooner or later!

History is replete with people who have defied incredible odds to accomplish unbelievable things. If you're one of those long shots like John Bertrand or Bo Eason, this book is for you. The stories I share and the studies I cite will redefine what is and what is not possible. But winning the day starts with redefining who you are and, more importantly, whose you are.

For better or for worse, our outlook on life is the by-product of a few experiences. I might add, *unanalyzed* experiences. Do you really think your seven-year-old self was capable of remembering the right way? Or your seventeen-year-old memories are spot on? I'm not even sure I remember *yesterday* the right way! Memory is both subjective and selective. If you don't believe me, just ask the fans of opposing teams to give you their opinions right after an instant replay! Memory is a lot like that. Subjective memories get blown out of proportion. Selective memories get subtracted from. And the way we weigh memory is often all out of whack.

A single failure can fashion a defeatist attitude.

A single trauma can amputate pieces of a personality.

A single rejection can destroy someone's capacity to trust.

My point? We need God to sanctify our memories as much as our imaginations.

HISTORICAL REVISIONISM

The story of the Exodus is Israel's signature story. It defined their identity as a free people. Even their calendar revolved around the day God delivered them. The anniversary of the Exodus, the Passover, was a day celebrated unlike any other. God delivered Israel in a single day, but they didn't possess the Promised Land until forty years later. Did you know that the entire journey from Mount Sinai to the Promised Land was supposed to take eleven days?[16] But they traveled for *forty years*! That's 14,589 days longer than their original ETA. What the heck happened?

Getting Israel out of Egypt was easy, relatively speaking. Getting Egypt out of Israel was a different story altogether, and I mean that literally. It took *one day* to get Israel out of Egypt, but it took *forty years* to get Egypt out of Israel. Why? When you've been enslaved for four hundred years, slavery is all you've ever known. Like the crew of *Australia II*, it was hard to imagine anything other than losing. When you've been oppressed for four hundred years, oppression has an epigenetic effect. You can't even imagine a different outcome, a different ending. Parting the Red Sea was simple compared with flipping Israel's script.

Just a few weeks after their miraculous deliverance, the Israelites started complaining about the manna. If I remember correctly, manna was a *miracle*. The Israelites were complaining about a *miracle*! Unbelievable, right? Not so fast. We fall into the same trap. Isn't marriage miraculous? Children? The human body? The human mind? I bet you've filed a few complaints about each of those.

The nation of Israel filed this official complaint: "We remember the fish we ate freely in Egypt and without cost, the cucumbers, melons, leeks, onions, and garlic."[17] *Seriously?* It was free because *you weren't*. Israel's problem—our problem—is selective memory. If you remember wrong, it's downright debilitating.

We don't see the world *as it is*. We see the world *as we are*. If you want to win today, you've got to start by rewriting yesterday.

When it comes to historiography, historical revisionism is the practice of reinterpreting past events. We need to put this into practice in our personal lives by remembering things the right way. How? From the far side of the cross! From the far side of the empty tomb! You aren't defined by the things you've done wrong. You are defined by what Christ did right—His righteousness. Jesus didn't just break the curse at Calvary's cross; He flipped the script on sin and death forever.

WHOSE YOU ARE

Four decades after the Exodus, the Israelites built an altar at a place called Gilgal. Altars are often the places where we bury dead yesterdays. The Lord said to Joshua, "Today I have rolled away the reproach of Egypt from you."[18] The Israelites were set free the moment they exited Egypt, but sometimes it takes forty years for the truth to catch up with us. Of course, the stigma of systemic racism takes much longer and is much harder to change.

In 1864, the year after the Emancipation Proclamation, Sojourner Truth visited the nation's capital and was shocked by the situation former slaves found themselves in. There were still 122 pages of black codes discriminating against them. Those codes imposed a curfew on people of color and disallowed black businesses. Black children weren't allowed to swim in the Anacostia River, sit on benches in Center Market, or fly kites on the National Mall.[19] Those codes were eventually changed, but the attitudes behind them and the experiences of them cannot be so easily rewritten. It's much easier rewriting laws than it is rewriting hearts—or stories for that matter!

A hundred years later, Dr. Martin Luther King Jr. delivered his "I Have a Dream" speech in the shadow of the Lincoln Memorial. Looking back on that day of deliverance, King said, "It came as a joyous daybreak to end the long night of their captivity."[20] Yes, it did, but the battle for civil rights had just begun!

When you've been enslaved for centuries, it takes time for your identity to catch up with your new reality. The battle is against the people and the powers actively working against your freedom—and the voice of doubt that calls your God-given dignity and identity into question. In the case of the Israelites, it took forty years. There are no shortcuts. There are no cheat codes. What God says about you has to become your signature story. It wasn't until the Israelites possessed the Promised Land that they finally saw themselves for who they really were—not slaves but God's chosen people.

Many of us see ourselves or see others the same way, according to some old code. There are plenty of people who want to remind us of those old narratives. You've got to let God flip the script. How? Scripture is a good starting point. The goal isn't getting through Scripture. It's getting Scripture through you. The Swiss theologian Karl Barth said, "Take your Bible and take your newspaper, and read both. But interpret newspapers from your Bible."[21] I would say the same of your everyday experiences. Over time, your theology conforms to your reality or your reality conforms to your theology. Scripture is more than our script; it's our script-cure. And that's more than a play on words. Scripture confronts the false identities and false narratives perpetrated by the Father of Lies. It reveals the heavenly Father's metanarrative and the unique role that each one of us plays in it.

Abraham thought he was *too old*. Jeremiah thought he was *too young*. Moses thought he was *unqualified*. Joseph thought he was *overqualified*. Gideon had *an inferiority complex*. Jonah had *a superiority complex*. Peter made *too many mistakes*. Nathanael was *too cool for school*. Paul had *a thorn in the flesh*. And King David was *the runt of the litter*.

None of that matters! *Who you are* is not the issue. What really matters is *whose you are*. If you are in Christ and Christ is in you, you are a new creation.[22] You are the apple of God's eye.[23] You are God's workmanship.[24] You are more than a conqueror, and nothing can change that.[25] It is what it is; it is who you are.

There never has been and never will be anyone like you. That isn't a testament to you. It's a testament to the God who created you. The significance of that truth is this: *no one can take your place*. No one can worship God like you or for you. No one can serve others like you or for you. Jesus doesn't just live *in us*; Christ lives *as us*!

Flip the script, and start living your life in a way that is worth telling stories about.

2

Ambidexterity

Your brave is someone else's breakthrough.

Joshua Haldeman grew up on the prairies of Saskatchewan. His first job was breaking wild broncos. With that acquired skill set, he would organize one of Canada's first rodeos. When the domino effect of the Great Depression hit Canada, Haldeman lost his five-thousand-acre farm and had to start from scratch. He tried his hand at chiropractic medicine and politics. Then Haldeman discovered his passion—flying airplanes.

In 1950, Haldeman uprooted his family and moved halfway around the world to South Africa, a place he had never even been to before! With the help of his wife, Winnifred, and their children, he disassembled his 1948 single-engine Bellanca Cruisair. The airplane was packed into crates, shipped to South Africa, and reassembled by the family once it got there.

A few years later, Joshua and Winnifred Haldeman embarked on a thirty-thousand-mile round-trip flight from Africa to Australia and back. They are believed to be the only private pilots to have ever made that flight in a single-engine airplane. As a comparison point, Charles Lindbergh's legendary transatlantic flight in 1927 was only 3,600 miles. Twenty-seven years later, the Haldemans flew more than eight times as far![1]

Few people have heard of Joshua and Winnifred Haldeman, but I bet you've heard of their grandson Elon Musk. Musk's entrepreneurial exploits are well documented. He has turned the automotive and aerospace industries upside down, ruffling a few feathers along the way. At SpaceX headquarters, there are two giant posters of Mars. One shows a cold, barren planet. The other looks a lot like Earth. The second poster represents Musk's life purpose—colonizing Mars. If that's not shooting for the moon, I'm not sure what is.

How does someone even conceptualize colonizing a planet, in the non-science-fiction sense? Who dreams that kind of interplanetary dream? I have a theory, and it has a lot to do with Elon Musk's genogram. Let's just say that the apple didn't fall far from Joshua Haldeman's tree! Dreams are not conceived in a vacuum. For better or for worse, each of us is born into someone else's story! "Throughout his childhood," noted one of Musk's biographers, "Elon heard many stories about his grandfather's exploits and sat through countless slide shows that documented his travels."[2] Those stories were the seedbed of Musk's imagination. Those stories were the shoulders he stood on.

Joshua Haldeman's signature story became a subplot in his grandson's story. I don't think Haldeman had any idea that his transcontinental flight would have an intergalactic ripple effect. But every move we make, every risk we take, sets the stage for someone else. Your brave is someone else's breakthrough. We think right here, right now. God is thinking nations and generations. We think that what God does for us is for us, but it's never just for us. It's always for the third and fourth generations. When we win the day, in our own unique way we enable future generations to dream a little bigger and think a little longer. Once you've flown thirty thousand miles in a single-engine plane, colonizing Mars isn't out of the question!

DELIBERATE PRACTICE

I'm fascinated by an ancient group of archers from a tribe known as the Benjamites. Their ambidextrous ability to shoot arrows and sling stones sounds like it's right out of a Marvel movie.

All of them were expert archers, and they could shoot arrows or sling stones with their left hand as well as their right. They were all relatives of Saul from the tribe of Benjamin.[3]

Their ability to use both hands equally well raises a few questions. Switch hitters are commonplace in baseball, but there is only one switch pitcher in Major League Baseball! I'm going to make an assumption that the Benjamites were not born this way. Only 1 percent of the population is born ambidextrous. In other words, this is *nurture over nature*. This was *not* an innate talent. It was a hard-earned skill set.

How did the Benjamites develop ambidexterity? And more importantly, why? Let me start with how, and then we'll explore why. There is only one way to become an expert archer: *lots of practice*. The ten-thousand-hour rule is often referred to, but it's also misinterpreted and misapplied. People falsely assume that it takes only ten thousand hours to achieve expertise in anything. But there's a catch: if you practice the right thing the wrong way, it's counterproductive. Doing something repeatedly won't give you the results you're looking for. This can be called naive practice, and it connotes half-hearted effort or half-minded focus. You develop bad habits while trying to build good habits. The key is something Anders Ericsson called "deliberate practice," and it's three-dimensional.[4]

The first dimension is *well-defined goals*. These allow you to measure progress, and they facilitate a feedback loop. The second dimension is *reverse engineering*. It's studying the best practices of others, then adopting them and adapting them to your unique situation. I already mentioned that I read three thousand books before writing one, but I did more than read them. I reverse engineered them, trying to figure out the tricks of the trade. The third dimension is *effort*. Deliberate practice requires near-maximal effort, which is neither fun nor easy. When you're training your body, you have to stress it beyond its ability to maintain homeostasis. For the record, this is *good* stress, or eustress. Anything less than 70 percent effort actually maintains the status quo.

You've got to attempt things that are just beyond your ability.[5] The technical term is *just manageable difficulty,* or JMD. It can't be so easy that you become bored or so difficult that you quit.

I have no idea what the Benjamite "CrossFit workout" looked like, but they got lots of blisters from drawing their bows. It took many years of deliberate practice for them to aim equally well with both eyes and both hands.

Anders Ericcson offered one more piece of advice when it comes to deliberate practice: "There is no point at which performance maxes out and additional practice does not lead to further improvement."[6] In other words, you never age out. Don't stop at ten thousand hours! Keep practicing till the day you die! That's what winning the day is all about.

METANARRATIVE

There are several famous Benjamites in the Bible, King Saul and the apostle Paul among them. Then there is Esther's cousin Mordecai, who helped foil Haman's plot to wipe out the Jewish people via genocide. The tribe of Benjamin has its fair share of heroes, but their George Washington is a judge named Ehud. Do you remember how Ehud delivered Israel? With his *left hand.*

> When the Israelites cried to the Lord, the Lord raised them up a deliverer, Ehud son of Gera, a Benjamite, a left-handed man.[7]

Ehud is one of the most significant southpaws in Scripture. So what? What does that have to do with the ambidexterity of the Benjamites? And why am I bringing Elon Musk into the mix?

The story of Ehud, the left-handed hero, wasn't just a narrative of the Benjamites. It was their metanarrative. Again, each of us is born into someone else's story. Just as Joshua Haldeman's legacy became part of Elon Musk's destiny, Ehud's left-handed victory became the Benjamites' signature story, buried deep within their collective consciousness. It was their rallying cry, like "Remember the Alamo!" Cultivating weak-hand skills was their unique way of honoring Ehud. Ambidexterity was a tip of the cap to the judge who delivered Israel with his left hand.

Most of us tend to ignore our nondominant hands. Why bother when using our strong hands is so much easier, so much better? We let our weak hands atrophy. But how you handle your weak hand affects more than your present task; it affects the next generation. Ehud didn't just deliver the Israelites from the Moabites; he inspired generations of Benjamites. His brave wasn't just their breakthrough; it became their signature story.

God wants to use you at your point of greatest giftedness. That's a given. He is the one who gave you those gifts in the first place. But God also wants to use you at your point of greatest weakness. Why? Because that is where His power is made perfect.[8] That is where we present double trouble to the Enemy.

What weakness do you need to work on? What skill set do you need to cultivate? Is there a story you need to take personally?

10x EFFORT

In his celebrated baseball book, *The Boys of Summer*, Roger Kahn profiled a Brooklyn Dodger named George "the Shotgun" Shuba. He described Shuba's swing as being "as natural as a smile."[9] Shuba laughed at Kahn's description, and I'll explain why in a moment.

During the off-season, Shuba would swing a weighted baseball bat six hundred times a day. And that was after working his off-season day job! Every evening, Shuba would take sixty swings, then mark an *X* on his swing chart. After ten rounds of sixty swings, Shuba would call it a night.

You've heard of 10x thinking? Instead of making 10 percent improvement, you target ten times improvement. You set goals that are ten times greater than what you think is possible. You take actions that are ten times greater than what you believe is necessary.

Long before Google started preaching 10x thinking, George Shuba was practicing 10x effort. That was Shuba's daily ritual for fifteen years, which brings us back to Roger Kahn calling his swing "as natural as a smile." "You call that natural?" Shuba asked Kahn. "I swung a 44-ounce bat 600 times a night, 4,200 times a week, 47,200 swings every winter."[10]

In my humble opinion, *there are no naturals*! Sure, some people are more naturally gifted than others. But unless that giftedness is coupled with a complementary work ethic, it'll result only in wasted potential. George "the Shotgun" Shuba swung his bat six hundred times a night, and I bet the Benjamites drew their bows at least 1,200 times a day. There is no other way to get good at shooting arrows. Their ambidexterity was evidence of 10x effort.

I can't help but wonder whether the other eleven tribes of Israel were just a little bit jealous of the Benjamites. I'm not sure they debated nature versus nurture back then, but they may have thought that the Benjamites had some kind of genetic advantage. I would argue otherwise. They put their pants on one leg at a time, just like the other tribes. Their advantage, if you can call it that, was a signature story. That signature story is what inspired their 10x effort.

SELF-FULFILLING PROPHECIES

According to some estimates, as many as 80 percent of our thoughts each day are negative.[11] If the battle is won or lost in the mind, that sounds like a losing battle before it's even begun! Flipping the script starts with your internal script. You can't let your inner critic—and we all have one—grab the mic and become the narrator! If you want to bury dead yesterdays, you've got to tune out the negative self-talk. How? Like the crew of *Australia II*, you have to rehearse a different story!

Gaylord Perry was a future Hall of Fame pitcher but a not-so-great batter. In 1964, his manager made an offhand comment: "Mark my words, a man will land on the moon before Gaylord Perry hits a home run." In one of the craziest coincidences in sports history, Perry hit the first home run of his twenty-two-year career on July 20, 1969, just minutes after the Apollo 11 lunar module landed on the moon.[12]

Self-fulfilling prophecies aren't always that specific or that dramatic, but Henry Ford was right: "Whether you believe you can do a thing or not, you are right."[13] For better or for worse, the stories we tell ourselves become self-fulfilling prophecies!

Consciously or subconsciously, we justify pieces of our personality and provide alibis for parts of our history. We excuse our character: *It's just the way I'm wired.* We maintain the status quo with these famous last words: *I've always done it that way.*

Can I ask an honest question? How is that working for you? *Your system is perfectly designed for the results you're getting!* If you want God to do something new, you can't keep doing the same old thing.

Everything is created twice. The first creation is always internal. More specifically, internal dialogue! The stories we tell ourselves eventually become the situations we find ourselves in. If you want to change your life, start by stewarding your story! How? You have to connect the dots.

CONNECT THE DOTS

Few phrases are more famous than *David versus Goliath*. It's the quintessential mismatch, the classic underdog story. The irony is that we read that story the wrong way. We think David was at a disadvantage. If it were hand-to-hand combat, yes! There is no way David could have defeated Goliath at Goliath's game. But David's biggest disadvantage, his lack of size, turned into his greatest advantage.

According to Eitan Hirsch, a ballistics expert with the Israeli Defense Forces, an average-sized stone slung by an expert could travel the length of a football field in three seconds flat. At that velocity, it would have the same stopping power as a .45-caliber handgun.[14] Goliath had a spear the size of a weaver's beam, and its tip weighed fifteen pounds.[15] That's awfully impressive, but Goliath brought a knife to a gunfight. David was *not* the underdog. Goliath was a sitting duck—and a really big one at that.

The irony of this story is that no one seemed to see David's potential. When the prophet Samuel came to anoint the next king of Israel, David's dad didn't even take him to the tryout. Talk about a father wound! Then when David volunteered to fight Goliath, Saul belittled him: "There's no way you can fight this Philistine and possibly win! You're only a boy, and he's been a man of war since his youth."[16]

David's response is like an ancient MRI. It gives us a glimpse of David's mindset. Here is what he said:

The LORD who delivered me from the paw of the lion and from the paw of the bear will deliver me from the hand of this Philistine.[17]

David was tending sheep on the sideline while his brothers were fighting on the front line. That had to be frustrating, but God was cultivating a skill set in David that would catapult him onto the national stage. God is doing the same thing in your life. What we perceive to be isolated incidents often prove to be inciting incidents that prepare us for future opportunities.

Every time you pass a test, you get a testimony. What is a testimony? It's evidence of God's past-tense providence in your life. Faith is connecting the dots between past-tense providence and present-tense circumstances. And, I might add, future-tense provision. Testimony is prophecy! If God did it before, He can do it again.

Right before this epic duel, King Saul offered David his armor. David could have gone into battle dressed like a king, quite literally. It was the best armor money could buy, but Saul's armor was not David's testimony. David's testimony was the slingshot he used to fend off bears and lions. Did David look a little foolish going into battle with a shepherd's sling? Sure he did, but faith is the willingness to look foolish. Who looked foolish afterward? At some point, you have to play to your strengths even if doing so feels foolish. That's how our brave becomes someone else's breakthrough.

If you fail to connect the dots between God's past-tense providence and your present-tense circumstances, the nine-foot giants in your life will seem like insurmountable problems. If you flip the script, you see nine-foot opportunities. Flipping the script will give you the courage to *run toward* rather than *run away* from the giants in your life. Why? You know that the battle belongs to the Lord. And the bigger they are, the harder they fall.

There is one final irony in this story: Saul was a *Benjamite.* If anyone was going to fight Goliath, it should have been him. Plus, he was head and shoulders taller than anyone else in Israel. What was the difference between David and Saul? David connected the dots, while Saul did not.

The lions and bears in each of our lives look different, but God is getting us ready to face the giants. Everything in your past is preparation for something in your future. It's the Goliath in front of us that helps us discover the David within us.

Origins of Genius

Some of the most successful people in the world have had to overcome the biggest giants. Some would argue that they achieved success *in spite of those odds,* but I would argue the opposite. I think they achieved success *because of them.* They had to overcome adversity by cultivating compensatory skills. They had to work a little harder to develop their weak hands, but that work ethic is what catapulted them to where they are today.

This may seem like a random fact, but I find it fascinating that no fewer than fifteen British prime ministers were orphaned before the age of sixteen.[18] Dean Keith Simonton wrote of parental loss in his book *Origins of Genius,* "Such adverse events nurture the development of a personality robust enough to overcome the many obstacles and frustrations standing in the path of achievement."[19]

All of us have odds to overcome, but those odds are not the enemy. Even Jesus had to overcome the odds and a negative narrative. "Can anything good come out of Nazareth?"[20] Jesus was from the wrong side of the tracks! We celebrate the Virgin Birth with something called Christmas, but the backstory of His birth cast a shadow on His identity, His legitimacy.

By his own admission, Elon Musk had a difficult childhood. He was bullied during high school, spending time in the hospital after getting pushed down the stairs and beaten until he blacked out. His home life wasn't much better. He described his childhood as "nonstop horrible."

One day, when he was ten years old, he saw a computer at an electronics store in Sandton City Mall in Johannesburg, South Africa. It was love at first sight. That Commodore VIC-20 had five kilobytes of memory and came with a workbook on the BASIC programming language. That language was supposed to take six months to acquire, but Musk learned it after three sleepless nights.[21] It was a new code, a new language, a new story. That code flipped his script, and he never looked back.

Could Elon Musk have learned to code without a challenging childhood? You bet. But he might not have pursued coding with the same kind of passion. Everything we experience is a two-sided coin. It can make us or break us, and that's up to us. You can get frustrated with the fact that you're right handed or left handed, or you can cultivate ambidexterity. You don't get to choose how your story starts, but the ending is up to you.

God can flip any script, and that includes David versus Goliath!

If you want to bury dead yesterdays, you've got to come to grips with who you are in Christ. False humility is thinking of yourself as anything less than who God says you are, and it's as destructive as pride. You may be up against a giant, but you are in Christ. And in Christ, you are nobody's underdog! Just like He did with David, God will turn your weakness into ambidextrous strength.

Your brave is someone else's breakthrough.

Your hurt is someone else's healing.

Your disappointment is someone else's deliverance.

One final footnote.

Do you know the best predictor of children's emotional well-being? It wasn't hugs and kisses, though I'm sure those help. It wasn't getting them into the best schools. It wasn't even taking them to see the latest and greatest Pixar film, though I'm sure that can't hurt! According to the researchers, a critical indicator of well-being is whether children know their family history![22] It was true for the Benjamites. It was true for David and the Son of David. I think it goes for all God's children!

If you don't know your family history, it's like skipping the first few pages of a book or the first few minutes of a movie. It's hard to see ourselves as a subplot. It's hard to locate the part we play in the story. The same is true spiritually. When you are born into the family of God, you get grafted into the story God has been writing since day one. That script is called Scripture, and it contains our family history. It's how we discover who the heavenly Father is. It's how we discover who we are as the children of God.

The Bible is your backstory. Your life is the rest of the story. In fact, you are the only Bible some people may ever read. Are you a good translation? The key, of course, is connecting the dots. If God did it before, He can do it again. If God did it for them, He can do it for you.

Flip the script.

Habit 2—Kiss the Wave

The obstacle is not the enemy;
the obstacle is the way.

On the day Sir William Osler delivered his address at Yale University, Wilder Penfield was sitting in the audience as a student. What inspiration he took from Osler's speech is unknown, but Penfield would discover just how difficult it is to bury dead yesterdays. Wilder Penfield would go on to study neuropathology at Oxford before setting up the Montreal Neurological Institute-Hospital.[1]

By the end of his illustrious career as a neurosurgeon, Dr. Penfield had explored the brains of 1,132 patients suffering from epileptic seizures. Using an instrument known as the Penfield dissector, he meticulously mapped the human brain. By stimulating different parts of the brain with a mild electrical current, Dr. Penfield found that his patients experienced vivid flashbacks of their past.

One patient recalled every note from a symphony she had heard at a concert many years before. The same spot was stimulated thirty times, and each time she remembered every note. Another patient recalled sitting at a train stop as a child, and she could describe each train car as it went by in her mind's eye. Not only were the flashbacks extremely detailed; some of them predated the patients' first conscious memories.

Dr. Penfield concluded that every sight, every sound, every smell—every experience that has once captured a person's attention—is somehow recorded on that person's internal hard drive, the cerebral cortex. Here's how it works. When you hear a song or see a picture, a line called an engram is traced on the surface of the cerebral cortex. If you hear the same song or see the same picture again, the line is retraced. With each repetition, the memory is more deeply ingrained until that song or picture is literally engraved on the surface of the cerebral cortex.

Our ability to remember the past is a gift from God, but it comes with a caveat. We don't always remember accurately. This fact reminds us that memory is both selective and subjective. As such, it can be a blessing and a curse. When we remember yesterday the wrong way, we live a lie. And living a lie undermines our ability to win the day.

Sometimes we misremember—or try to forget—because the past can be incredibly painful. That's where the second habit—*kiss the wave*—comes into play. You've got to own the past, or the past will own you. How? You have to accurately inventory your past, hiding from nothing. Then you have to own all of it—the good, the bad, and the ugly. It is what it is. Or maybe I should say, it is what it *was*. You may not be *responsible* for what happened, but you are *response-able*.

Two people can encounter the same obstacle—a difficult diagnosis, a bitter divorce, or even the death of a loved one—yet come out on the other side very different people. One person owns his or her pain, while the other person is owned by it. One person becomes better, while the other person becomes bitter. The difference? You've got to kiss the wave that throws you against the Rock of Ages. You've got to come to terms with the pain that has made you who you are.

God comes to us disguised as our lives! Every circumstance, from the greatest of joys to the deepest of sorrows, is an opportunity to discover new dimensions of God's character. Instead of trying to change the past, which is impossible, what if we leveraged its lessons to change ourselves? Any obstacle you encounter is not the enemy; the obstacle is the way.

It's time to kiss the wave!

3

The Obstacle Is the Way

You may not be responsible, but you are response-able.

J oseph Merrick was born in Leicester, England, on August 5, 1862. It's
difficult to properly diagnose someone who predates modern medicine, but few people have suffered from more physical deformities. All
ten of his fingers were useless stubs. His misshapen head was the cir-
cumference of a man's waist. His distorted mouth made his speech almost unintelligible. His right arm was twice the size of his left arm, and
his deformed legs could barely support his weight.

In nineteenth-century England, a perverse yet popular form of en-
tertainment was human novelty exhibitions. Joseph Merrick was the
headliner in one of these exhibits. Posters pronounced him half-man,
half-elephant. People paid their shillings to see the human freak show,
then shrieked in horror at the sight of him.

One day, a surgeon named Frederick Treves wandered into the
human circus. His assessment of Joseph Merrick was similar to everyone else's: "[He was] the most disgusting specimen of humanity that I
had ever seen."[1] But Dr. Treves didn't shriek and shrink away. Merrick's
physical appearance piqued his scientific curiosity—and no small measure of empathy. The good doctor tried talking to Merrick, but he wasn't
able to decipher his speech. He did, however, hand him his business
card. It was that business card that London police found on his person

when they discovered Merrick huddled in a dark corner of a train station, looking like a wounded animal. The police called Dr. Treves, and Dr. Treves took Merrick to the London Hospital, where he would spend the remainder of his life.

Shortly after Merrick's arrival, Dr. Treves ordered a tray of food for him, but he failed to warn the orderly who delivered it. When she saw Merrick, she dropped the tray and ran out of the room, screaming. Over time, however, the hospital staff became accustomed to his peculiar appearance.

One day, in a carefully orchestrated experiment, Dr. Treves arranged to have a woman enter Merrick's room, smile at him, wish him good morning, and shake his hand. Dr. Treves recorded what he witnessed:

> The effect upon poor Merrick was not quite what I had expected. As he let go her hand he bent his head on his knees and sobbed until I thought he would never cease. . . . He told me afterwards that this was the first woman who had ever smiled at him, and the first woman, in the whole of his life, who had shaken hands with him.[2]

That smile proved to be the tipping point, the turning point. "He began to change, little by little, from a hunted thing into a man."[3] Dr. Treves listened to Merrick long enough and hard enough to finally decipher his garbled speech. He found Merrick to be both intelligent and articulate. A voracious reader of Scripture, Merrick had a holy curiosity that encompassed all of life. Dr. Treves smuggled him into the private boxes of London theaters to watch plays and listen to operas. He gave him books to read. He took him into the countryside, where Merrick loved listening to songbirds, chasing rabbits, and picking wildflowers. More than once, he remarked, "I am happy every hour of the day."[4]

After Merrick's death at age twenty seven, Dr. Treves eulogized the infamous Elephant Man this way: "His troubles had ennobled him. He showed himself to be a gentle, affectionate and lovable creature . . .

without a grievance and without an unkind word for anyone. I have never heard him complain."[5]

Never heard him complain? How is that even possible with the kind of trauma he experienced? *Happy every hour of the day?* How does someone who was mistreated for so many years profess happiness every hour of the day?

The answer is the second habit—*kiss the wave.* You may not be *responsible* for the difficulties you've had to endure, but you are *response-able.* At the end of the day, your *explanations* are more important than your *experiences.* Joseph Merrick is exhibit A. It's incredibly counterintuitive, but the obstacles we encounter are *not* the enemy. The enemy, more often than not, is *us.* The obstacle? The obstacle—believe it or not—is the way.

KISS THE WAVE

I have a friend who has had a migraine for five years. Moments of relief are few and far between. The pain became so debilitating that he eventually had to resign from the church he was pastoring. He's been to countless specialists. He's tried a wide variety of treatment plans. Nothing seems to help much or for long.

I asked him how he's managed the pain and the emotions that go with it. He said, "I've learned to kiss the wave." I must have given him a quizzical look, so my friend explained. He was quoting Charles Spurgeon: "I have learned to kiss the wave that throws me against the Rock of Ages."[6]

It's a powerful sentence all by itself, but the backstory makes it even more meaningful. Before I unpack the whole story, let me say something point blank. Kissing the wave doesn't mean we don't experience storms or get seasick during them. The good news? There is a God who can rebuke the wind and the waves with these words: "Peace, be still."[7] But before you rebuke the storm, you need to accept it. You can't move past the pain if you ignore it or hide it or deny it.

A few years ago, Lora and I found ourselves thrown against the Rock of Ages. Lora was diagnosed with breast cancer. If you've had cancer or have a loved one who has, you know that a thousand questions fire across your synapses. *What stage is it? How do we treat it? What is the prognosis?* Fortunately, we caught it early and Lora is better than ever.

Can I brag on my wife? I don't think I've ever been prouder of her. Lora kissed the wave. How? She participated in her own healing process by making some courageous changes. She became intentional about everything she put in her body and in her mind. Along with changing our diet, we did our best to eliminate toxins in our environment. Yes, that includes people. Lora started practicing meditation more regularly. We even started frequenting comedy clubs. Why? Laughter "doeth good like a medicine."[8]

When you get cancer, denying the diagnosis does no good. If you don't own it, it will own you. Kissing the wave is confessing what's wrong—in this case, cancer. But it's also professing what's right—God's healing power. Remember my miraculous healing from asthma? It began with *a brave prayer.* For Lora, the healing process began with *a brave question* she stumbled across while reading a poem about illness:

What have you come to teach me?

When we find ourselves in difficult situations, we get so focused on getting out of them that we fail to get anything out of them. Then we wonder why we find ourselves in the same situation all over again. There is nothing wrong with asking God to change your circumstances, but His primary objective is changing *you.* The circumstances you're asking God to change may be the very circumstances He is using to change you.

In the words of John Piper, "Don't waste your cancer."[9] You can fill in the blank with whatever challenge you face. Don't waste it! Maybe it has come to teach you a lesson that could not be learned any other way! Kissing the wave starts with a brave question: *What have you come to teach me?*

You don't need to sabotage yourself—that's for sure. Suffering will find you soon enough. When it does, you must recognize that it has the power to enrich your life in a way that nothing else can. If you find yourself in a season of suffering, that is a difficult sentence to read. I acknowledge that, and I don't stand in judgment over others, because I don't stand in their shoes. I don't pretend to know the trauma you've endured. I do know this: *everyone is fighting a battle we know nothing about.*

Lora and I have experienced our fair share of grief and pain and disappointment. I'm not sure where we rank on the bell curve, especially compared with those who have experienced injustice or aren't sure where their next meals are coming from. Like our memories, suffering is subjective. We have some long-lasting regrets, like every parent I know. We have deep wells of sadness, like every person I know. We have walked through the valley of the shadow of death more than once, and we have the emotional scars to prove it. We've also seen God turn some of our toughest tests into our most treasured testimonies. We wouldn't want to live those seasons all over again, but we wouldn't trade them for anything in the world. Every *testimony* starts with *test*. Pass the test, and you get a testimony, and testimony is the way you overcome the next obstacle!

At this point, you may think this book has taken a wrong turn. I assure you, it has not. The first few chapters are the toughest to read because they focus on the hardest habits to cultivate. If you were looking for a quick fix, you came to the wrong place. If you want to win the day, you've got to kiss the wave.

Flashback

On October 19, 1856, Charles Spurgeon was preaching to ten thousand people in London's Surrey Gardens Music Hall when someone yelled "Fire!" It was pure pandemonium. Those trying to get into the building blocked those trying to get out. A balcony collapsed beneath the stampede. By the time the commotion was quelled, seven people had died and twenty-eight were seriously injured.

Spurgeon's text that night was Proverbs 3:33: "The curse of the Lord is in the house of the wicked."[10] He would never preach that passage again. In fact, the man commonly referred to as the Prince of Preachers came close to never preaching again, period. For quite some time, the very sight of the Bible caused Charles Spurgeon to cry. When he finally stepped back into the pulpit where he had last preached, painful emotions flooded his soul, and they never went away. Twenty-five years after the Surrey Hall disaster, Spurgeon was speaking to a gathering of the Baptist Union when something about the setting triggered a flashback that left him speechless for many minutes.

At the time of the tragedy, Charles Spurgeon was only twenty-two years old. He was the newly installed pastor of what would become the largest church in the world, Metropolitan Tabernacle. Plus, he was ten months married with twin boys who were days old.

I did a quick calculation based on the Social Readjustment Rating Scale.[11] Spurgeon scored 358, by my count. Anything over 300 on that stress test indicates an 80 percent chance of illness in the near future. I would add mental illness to the mix. And that stress test doesn't even account for the fact that London newspapers were blaming Spurgeon for the tragedy.

How do you flip that script?

How do you kiss that wave?

Few people have advanced the kingdom of God quite like Charles Spurgeon. Along with pastoring the largest church in the world, he wrote 150 books, started a college, and led sixty-six charities. Makes me wonder what he did during all his spare time!

Despite his many successes, Spurgeon was marked by melancholy. It took a measure of courage to admit his thorn in the flesh, but he did not keep secret his many bouts with deep depression. Like my friend who suffers from migraines, Spurgeon experienced few remissions from depression.

My spirits were sunken so low that I could weep by the hour like a child, and yet I knew not what I wept for.[12]

"Grief is depression in proportion to circumstance," said Dr. Andrew Solomon. Grief is a good thing, a God thing. God is the one who created us with tear ducts. But emotions like grief can be inflated or deflated just like our memories. That's when we endanger ourselves with our own emotions. In Dr. Solomon's words, "Depression is grief out of proportion to circumstance."[13]

Go ahead and grieve. It's one way we kiss the wave. Like physical wounds, if emotional wounds don't fully heal, they can become infected. If you try to shortcut grief, it will short-circuit your soul. But you can't get stuck in the stages of grief—in denial or anger or bargaining or depression. Somehow, someway, you've got to accept your new normal and find new meaning.[14] The good news? We don't grieve as those who have no hope![15]

THE BEST OF TIMES, THE WORST OF TIMES

A few years after the Surrey Hall tragedy, a contemporary of Charles Spurgeon, Charles Dickens, wrote *A Tale of Two Cities*.

It was the best of times, it was the worst of times, it was the age of wisdom, it was the age of foolishness, it was the epoch of belief, it was the epoch of incredulity, it was the season of Light, it was the season of Darkness, it was the spring of hope, it was the winter of despair.

More than just an epic opening, it's a truthful take on life. We want the best of times without the worst. We want wisdom without foolishness, light without darkness, hope without despair. That isn't reality, is it? The best of times and the worst of times often occur at the same time! Life is a two-sided coin.

In 1974, Stephen Colbert lost his father and two brothers in a plane crash. Stephen was only ten years old. His world was shattered.[16] In an interview with Anderson Cooper, Colbert discussed his belief that he had to learn to "love the thing that I most wish had not happened." That almost seems wrong, right? Colbert explained that sentiment:

> It's a gift to exist, and with existence comes suffering. There's no escaping that. I don't want it to have happened. I want it to *not* have happened, but if you are grateful for your life—which I think is a positive thing to do, not everybody is, and I am not always but it's the most positive thing to do—then you have to be grateful for all of it. You can't pick and choose what you're grateful for.[17]

That's a tough pill to swallow, but that's kissing the wave.

BLAMING GOD

Remember Joseph Merrick?

How does someone who is misunderstood and mistreated for so many years consider himself blessed, not cursed? Become a better version of himself rather than a bitter soul? The secret is a poem Merrick is said to have frequently repeated:

> Tis true, my form is something odd
> But blaming me, is blaming God,
> Could I create myself anew
> I would not fail in pleasing you.[18]

It's not just beauty that is in the eye of the beholder. Everything is! You can blame God for this, that, and the other thing. And I certainly don't profess innocence on that count. Lots of things don't make sense to me, and I've put God on trial a few times.

On January 6, 1998, my fifty-five-year-old father-in-law died from a heart attack. It was a total shock, and it shook our family to the core. The compass needle still spins. I don't understand why God would allow that to happen. He was in the prime of life, the prime of ministry. Shortly thereafter, I was reading Deuteronomy 29:29. It says that the revealed things belong to us but the secret things belong to God. That's when I created what I have come to call my Deuteronomy 29:29 file. That file is full of things that don't make sense to Mark. It consists of questions that won't get answered on this side of eternity, and it's getting awfully thick.

If you find yourself in a season of suffering, it raises lots of questions. If it's a divorce—*Will I ever find true love?* If it's a difficult diagnosis— *What is my new normal?* If it's a dream that's died—*What do I do now?* I can't answer those questions. But if you lean in and learn to kiss the wave, you can come out on the other side stronger and kinder and wiser. It won't be easy and it won't be painless. It's those unanswered questions, unresolved mysteries, and unsettled situations that cause many people to blame God. As hard as it is, I have nowhere else to turn but to the Rock of Ages.

Sometimes God delivers us *from* suffering. More often than not, He delivers us *through* it. Why? So we can help others. That's precisely what Charles Spurgeon did. "Hundreds of times I have been able to give a helpful grip to brethren and sisters who have come into that same condition, which grip I could never have given if I had not known their deep despondency."[19]

Deriving pleasure from pain is masochism, not sanctification. Kissing the wave is simply acknowledging that *it is what it is.* You have to own what happened without letting it own your emotions. Kissing the wave is not obsessive compulsive or passive aggressive. Kissing the wave is the Serenity Prayer, penned by Reinhold Niebuhr:

God, grant me the serenity to accept the things I cannot change, courage to change the things I can and wisdom to know the difference.[20]

If you want to bury a dead yesterday, you've got to take response-ability for it. The key, of course, is the hyphen. It may not be your fault. That doesn't change the fact that you are able to choose your response in every situation.

Did you know that there is more to the Serenity Prayer than the sentence I just cited? The rest of Niebuhr's prayer harmonizes with Osler's day-tight compartments. For the record, Niebuhr graduated from Yale University in 1914, so I wouldn't be surprised if he heard Osler's speech.

> Living one day at a time,
> Enjoying one moment at a time,
> Accepting hardship as a pathway to peace,
> Taking, as Jesus did,
> This sinful world as it is,
> Not as I would have it,
> Trusting that You will make all things right,
> If I surrender to Your will,
> So that I may be reasonably happy in this life,
> And supremely happy with You forever in the next.[21]

Holy Best

In his memoir *The Sacred Journey*, Frederick Buechner wrote about the effect that his father's suicide had on him as a young boy. It was devastating. If you've experienced that kind of trauma, you never get over it. But you can get through it with God's help. Buechner described the healing process this way:

> When it comes to putting broken lives back together . . . the human best tends to be at odds with the holy best. To do for yourself the best that you have it in you to do—to grit your teeth and clench your fists in order to survive the world at its harshest

and worst—is, by that very act, to be unable to let something be done for you and in you that is more wonderful still.[22]

Kathleen Norris once observed, "Modern believers tend to trust in therapy more than in mystery."[23] There is nothing wrong with therapy! I've never met anyone who couldn't use some counseling, and I've benefited from it tremendously! Healing happens where therapy meets mystery.

There is a song that I put on repeat during difficult seasons of life. It's Martin Luther's magnum opus, "A Mighty Fortress Is Our God." The second verse opens with this statement: "Did we in our own strength confide, our striving would be losing." Your best isn't good enough, and that's okay. The last line of that verse points us back to the One who is good enough—Jesus Christ. "He must win the battle."[24] And He has!

Relying on God's grace is no easier than relying on God for daily bread. We want to be self-sufficient. In fact, we confuse self-sufficiency with spiritual maturity. Our only sufficiency is the grace of God, and the only way we qualify for it is that we don't. His grace has the power to bury dead yesterdays six feet deep! The problem, of course, is that we dig them back up!

Religion is spelled *do. Christianity* is spelled *done.* It's not about what you can do for God. It's about what God has done for you at Calvary's cross. Jesus said, "It is finished."[25] That's how we bury dead yesterdays. We nail them to the cross. Then we take up our cross and carry it daily.[26]

There is an old axiom: "Let go and let God." It's hard to let go of present-tense concerns and future-tense anxieties, but nothing is harder than letting go of past-tense pain. How do we let go? We own it so it doesn't own us! We take full response-ability for everything in our lives. We learn pain's lessons by asking a brave question: *What have you come to teach me?*

Kiss the wave!

4

Postimagining

Your explanations are more important
than your experiences.

In 1911, a Swiss psychologist named Édouard Claparède was treating a forty-seven-year-old patient with no short-term memory. At the beginning of every appointment, they would shake hands. Then one day, Claparède decided to perform a little experiment. When his patient reached out her hand, he had a pin concealed in his hand. Upon feeling the painful pinprick, the patient quickly withdrew her hand. A few minutes later, she had no memory of the pinprick. Yet from that day forward, she would not shake hands with Claparède. She wasn't sure why, but she felt like she couldn't completely trust him. The residue of pain kept her from reaching out. That's true of many of us, and it's true in many ways!

A few years before Édouard Claparède's pinprick, a Russian physiologist named Ivan Petrovich Pavlov performed a groundbreaking experiment that would win him the Nobel Prize. Dogs naturally salivate when presented with food, but Pavlov wanted to see whether salivation could be caused by another stimulus. As you may remember from a high school science class, Pavlov conditioned a dog by sounding a buzzer before feeding it. Eventually, the buzzer, even without the presence of food, was enough to cause salivation. This learned response is often referred to as a conditioned reflex.

To one degree or another, all of us are Pavlovian. We have been consciously and subconsciously conditioned our entire lives, and much of our behavior is dictated by those conditioned reflexes. Claparède's patient who would not shake his hand because of a forgotten pinprick is a classic example.

Every time I fill up my gas tank, I instinctively look in the side-view mirror before driving off. Why? Because I once ripped a gas hose right out of a gas pump! It ranks as one of the most embarrassing moments of my life! I was wondering why everyone was waving at me as I pulled out of the gas station. Awfully friendly, these people! No, they were afraid that the sparks from the hose that I was dragging behind my car would cause a fire!

I have filled up my gas tank hundreds of times since then without incident. It doesn't matter. I still have this subconscious feeling that I forgot to remove the hose. For me, double-checking the side-view mirror is a conditioned reflex.

Over the course of our lifetimes, we acquire an elaborate repertoire of conditioned reflexes. Some of them are minor idiosyncrasies, like a nervous laugh. Others become major personality traits, like sarcasm. Some conditioned reflexes are as natural and normal as a blush. Others are as destructive as cutting or bingeing. One thing is certain: we are far more conditioned than we realize.

One half of winning the day is learning what we don't know. The other half is unlearning what we do know. You tell me: Which is harder? Kissing the wave is owning your past so it doesn't own you. It's understanding that the obstacle is the way. But kissing the wave is also kissing it goodbye!

THE MISS HAVISHAM EFFECT

Remember Prince Albert? In the same year that he died, Charles Dickens published a book titled *Great Expectations*. He wrote about a wealthy spinster named Miss Havisham whose wedding day turned into a nightmare. The love of her life, Compeyson, was a no-show. Even worse, he feigned love to defraud her.

Humiliated and heartbroken, Miss Havisham had a mental breakdown. Not unlike Queen Victoria wearing black clothing the rest of her life, Miss Havisham never took off her white wedding gown. The offense that broke her heart took place at forty minutes past eight o'clock in the morning. Time stood still, quite literally. Unfortunately, not in the same way it did for Tony Campolo on top of the Empire State Building. She stopped all the clocks in her house at that precise time. She got stuck in a moment, and she couldn't get out of it. Even if her clocks were correct twice a day, she lived the rest of her life in past-tense pain.

I wish that Miss Havisham were nothing more than a figment of Charles Dickens's imagination, but we all know that she is not. We all know a Miss Havisham or feel a little bit like her. We all know someone who hasn't died but who's stopped living. A traumatic experience holds that person hostage, and the ransom is the rest of his or her life. Like Miss Havisham, we often employ coping strategies that are counterproductive. Do you know why Queen Victoria rarely went outside? In part, because she was embarrassed by the weight she put on after Albert's death. Comfort food was her coping mechanism.

If you want to win the day, you've got to self-scout. You've got to identify the ways in which you sabotage yourself, then interrupt those unhealthy patterns. In psychological circles, *the Miss Havisham effect* refers to being psychologically stuck because of lost love. Few things are harder to overcome, and the more you love, the more it hurts. That's where a relationship with God enters the equation.

"The secret to intimacy with another person," said Craig Barnes, "is discovering the sufficiency of God's love without that person."[1] Contrary to what Jerry Maguire said to Dorothy Boyd, you don't complete me![2] No one can, save Christ. Our sufficiency is Christ alone. His love sets us free to be who we were meant to be.

When you know that you are loved by God, you don't have to play

God. And the people you love don't have to bear that impossible burden either.

RELEASE THE SCAR TISSUE

During my sophomore season in college, I tore my anterior cruciate ligament in the last game of the national basketball tournament. An orthopedic surgeon did reconstructive knee surgery a few weeks later. It took about nine months to regain full strength. It took a lot longer to regain full confidence cutting to the basket.

Two years after that injury, I was named a first-team all-American. Don't be overly impressed; it was *not* the NCAA. It was the NCCAA— the extra *C* stands for *Christian*. It's a nice story line, but here's the reality. My knee has never been the same. Between both knees, I've had six surgeries. Yes, I have biked centuries and run marathons. But I've had to find a new normal, which involves ibuprofen now and then.

When we experience physical trauma, our bodies form scar tissue. Unlike our original tissue, scar tissue develops in random patterns. The result is a loss of functionality. In my case, a loss of flexibility. I never regained my full range of motion, and I take full responsibility for that fact. I didn't do what the physical therapist told me to do! She told me that I needed to *release the scar tissue.* How? By massaging it. If you don't release the scar tissue, it becomes a weak link in the kinetic chain. Instead of tension being evenly distributed across a muscle group, scar tissue causes unhealthy tension. If that scar tissue is not released, it opens you up to reinjury.

What's true of physical trauma is true of emotional, relational, and spiritual trauma. We form scar tissue around old injuries. If we don't have the coping mechanism to deal with the trauma, we often resort to defense mechanisms that may protect us from pain but may not promote long-term healing.

When someone you trust causes trauma, it leaves a scar. If you don't forgive that person, the trauma builds up as bitterness. I don't want to oversimplify how difficult forgiveness can be. There are no simple solutions or easy answers. But the way you release scar tissue, spiritually speaking, is through forgiveness. If you don't release that scar tissue, you lose emotional range of motion—the ability to experience joy, the ability to experience intimacy. While we're on the subject, let me flip the script. We must take a trauma-informed approach with those who have experienced racial injustice, sexual harassment, or any other wound that is easily triggered. Anything less adds insult to injury.

Good for the Soul

Several years ago, I was invited to speak at a symposium in Wittenberg, Germany. That is where Martin Luther posted his Ninety-Five Theses on the doors of Castle Church, catalyzing the Protestant Reformation. I decided to research Luther by reading a biography, and the thing that struck me most is the fact that he would spend up to six hours at a time in confession. I couldn't remember the last time I had spent six minutes! Did Martin Luther have more to confess than me? I seriously doubt it. Maybe Luther knew something about the power of confession that eludes most of us.

Lord, forgive me for everything I've ever done wrong. I have no doubt that God can answer that prayer, but in my opinion, it's weak sauce. And the feeling of being forgiven will probably last about six seconds!

Our confessions of sin need to be as well defined as our professions of faith. If faith is being sure of what we hope for, then repentance is being sure of what we're sorry for. If it helps, try a written confession.

The less we confess, the less forgiven we feel.

The more we confess, the more forgiven we feel.

The old adage is true: "Confession is good for the soul." Whatever you don't confess, you repress. And whatever you repress eventually resurfaces in ways that are unhealthy and unholy, often at the most inopportune times!

If you want forgiveness to sink a little deeper into your soul, try confessing a little longer. That doesn't mean beating yourself up for six hours. It's giving the Holy Spirit elbow room to work in the deep places of your soul. The standard counseling session lasts about fifty minutes. If you give the Counselor that kind of time, I have no doubt you'll kiss the wave.

TWO TYPES OF IMAGINATION

Leonardo Da Vinci made a distinction between two types of imagination: *preimagining* and *postimagining*.[3] Preimagining, as you can probably deduce from the prefix, is *imagining the future before it happens.* We'll practice preimagining in part 3 when we imagine unborn tomorrows.

We generally think of imagination in future-tense terms, but all parents of preschoolers know that kids have imaginative memories too. Especially when it comes to the proverbial cookie jar! True or false, postimagining is *reimagining the past after it happens*! This is when many of us make excuses or provide alibis for the hand that got caught in that cookie jar. But let me flip the script. This is also how we acknowledge the hand of God. Isn't that what David did with the lions and the bears? He postimagined his past from a providential point of view.

When I started preaching, I was frustrated by the fact that I wasn't good at speaking extemporaneously. I had to script every word, every time. Speaking from an outline would have been much easier, but it wasn't in my wheelhouse. I had no idea at the time, but God was honing my writing. What I perceived to be a speaking weakness turned into a writing strength.

Alfred Adler would call it a compensatory skill. Perceived disadvantages, like David's size, often prove to be well-disguised advantages. How? They force us to develop attitudes and abilities that would have gone undiscovered otherwise. Once again, the obstacle is the way! It's as we compensate for our weak hands that we discover some of our greatest ambidextrous gifts.

The way we interpret history is a function of personality, theology, and even genealogy. Sometimes we romanticize the past, looking at it through rose-colored glasses. Can I make a confession as a former college athlete? *The older I get, the better I was!* I know I'm not alone! Of course, we also catastrophize the past, magnifying the hardships we've faced.

My grandparents may have gone to school the old-fashioned way—walking. But it definitely wasn't uphill both ways! My point? Our recollections are not objective. They're as subjective as our favorite foods, our favorite songs, and our favorite colors. Each of us connects the dots in our own unique way. Then we paint that picture of the past like an impressionist. That impressionist painting is the backdrop against which we view the present and the future.

The Body Keeps the Score

In his *New York Times* bestseller, *The Body Keeps the Score,* Bessel van der Kolk told the story of a modern-day Miss Havisham. A twenty-eight-year-old nurse's aide went to see a doctor about a 408-pound problem—her weight. Over the course of fifty-one weeks, she lost more than half her body weight. She dropped 276 pounds, getting all the way down to 132 pounds. Then she regained a shocking amount of weight in just a few months, leaving her doctor perplexed.

The woman identified obesity as her problem, but presenting problems are rarely the root of our issues. After she lost all that weight, a colleague made an unwanted sexual advance. That incident triggered repressed pain, and this woman ended up revealing to her doctor a lengthy history of sexual abuse by her grandfather.

How did she deal with her pain? She ate almost every waking moment. Why? Obesity was a defense mechanism to keep others at bay.[4] When this woman was made to feel as helpless as she had been as a little girl, eating was the only coping mechanism she had.

Each of us has a unique repertoire of complex coping mechanisms. Some people, like this woman, eat to become invisible. Others drink to drown their sorrows. And some sabotage their success because of deep-seated shame. I know the pain is as real as the events that occurred, but you are still response-able. I hope that empowers you. With God's grace, you can kiss the wave. How? You've got to evaluate—and perhaps reinvent—your coping mechanisms. I ask this question with genuine empathy: *How are your coping mechanisms working for you?* If they are causing negative side effects, it's time to try a different technique.

Trauma is not one size fits all, and neither is the healing process. But healing often starts with the courageous decision to confess the hurt. And not just the presenting problem. You've got to get to the root.

One of the most remarkable miracles in the Gospels involved a man who had not taken a single step in thirty-eight years. Jesus asked him what seems like a heartless question: "Do you want to get well?"[5] That seems a little insulting, doesn't it? Not so fast. I know people—and you do too—who don't want to get well. They would rather die than change. If you don't want to get well, even Jesus can't heal you. That's true even if the pain that put you there was not your fault. If you're going to flip the script, the pain of staying the same has to be greater than the pain of change.

Do I believe in divine healing? How can I not after God healed my asthma? But let me tell you what I did not do when God healed me. I did *not* start smoking! All too often, we undermine our own healing instead of participating in it.

God can deliver in a day, no doubt. But you've got to back up that deliverance with daily habits that fortify your newfound freedom. If you don't, it'll be short lived. You'll end up right back where you started—or worse. That's not a threat; it's a reality check. When Jesus healed the man who hadn't walked in thirty-eight years, healing came with a warning: "Stop sinning or something worse may happen to you."[6]

Is there something you need to stop?

Why are you waiting?

Mock Funeral

In 2002, Steve Jobs staged a famous mock funeral at Apple's annual conference for developers. A coffin was brought onstage at the San Jose Convention Center. The sound system started playing Bach's Toccata and Fugue in D Minor. After a moment of silence, Steve Jobs eulogized the operating system OS 9. "Today we say farewell to OS 9 for all future development," said Jobs, "and we focus our energies on developing Mac OS X."[7]

Is there something you need to bury?

Maybe it's time for a mock funeral.

After the infamous Monday Night Massacre—a 45–3 loss by the New York Jets to the New England Patriots on December 6, 2010—Coach Rex Ryan took a page out of Steve Jobs's playbook. Ryan dug a hole next to the practice field, and he took the entire football team through a mock funeral. He buried a football and, with it, the memory of that humiliating loss. Six weeks later, the Jets rebounded to beat the Patriots in a playoff game.

Before flipping the page on the past, you have to give dead yesterdays a proper burial. When God told Jacob to return to Bethel twenty years after his life-altering dream, Jacob experienced a full-circle moment. He had processed his past, as evidenced by his name change. Jacob was now Israel. What did he do next? He built an altar, but that's not all. He held a mock funeral. His family handed over the pagan idols they had accumulated, and Jacob buried them beneath the oak tree at Shechem.[8] Why the oak tree at Shechem? Why not? That is where Abraham first built an altar to God more than a century before.[9] It was holy ground. I think Jacob was connecting the dots, just like David.

I'm not sure what you need to bury or how you need to do so. Be careful not to shortcut the grieving process, or you could short-circuit the healing process. But at some point, you've got to get past the past. You've got to get on with the business of living. If it helps, hold a funeral.

With the help of the Holy Spirit, do some postimagining. You don't have to rewrite your entire autobiography, but take time to identify your signature story and subplots. What are the themes God is writing in your life? What compensatory skills has God been cultivating in you? How have past adversities prepared you for present opportunities?

Can I play life coach and help you identify your defining moments?

Look at your past chronologically and relationally. First, divide your life into chapters based on ages and stages. What are your earliest memories? What were the turning points and tipping points in elementary school, junior high, and high school? Once you get past college, you can use geography or jobs to divide your life into seasons. What decisions altered your trajectory? Who left their fingerprints on your soul during different stages of life? What mistakes do you most regret? What accomplishments are you most proud of? Which days would you like to live all over again? Which days were the most difficult, and why? What are the hardest lessons you've learned along the way? I know that's the tip of the iceberg, but I hope it points you in the right direction.

Epic Failures

There are quite a few epic failures in Scripture, but none is more rehearsed than Peter's denial of Jesus. Jesus even gave him a warning! "This very night, before the rooster crows, you will deny me three times."[10] Could Jesus have been any more specific? Yet Peter denied Jesus a third time right as the rooster crowed.

Remember Ivan Pavlov? Here's a Pavlovian thought as it relates to Peter: *I wonder whether Peter felt a twinge of guilt every time he heard a rooster crow.* Have you ever noticed the way sensory stimuli can trigger old memories? Seemingly insignificant sights and sounds and smells can evoke powerful emotions! Whenever I smell lilacs, for example, I'm transported across time and space to my grandparents' garden in Fridley, Minnesota. In much the same way, the sound of a rooster's crow had to have had a physiological effect on Peter—an auditory reminder of his epic failure.

This story is difficult for urbanites like me to imagine because the rooster population in Washington, DC, is zero. It wasn't until I woke up on Isabela Island in the Galápagos Islands that I appreciated the full effect a rooster's crow must have had. I woke up to a rooster choir right outside my window—with no snooze button.

Every morning, Peter was rudely awakened by a reminder of his epic failure. That's the way the Enemy works, right? He's the accuser of the brethren.[11] He wants to constantly remind you of everything you've done wrong. He doesn't just prowl like a roaring lion;[12] he crows like a rooster. The good news? God can recondition your reflexes with His grace.

It's much easier to *act* like a Christian than it is to *react* like one. Am I right? Most of us are good actors! We play the part pretty well—until we hit rush hour traffic. Or is that just me? It's our reactions that reveal who we really are. And maybe that is why Jesus focused so much of His teaching on reconditioning reflexes.

Pray for those who persecute you.[13]

Love your enemies.[14]

Bless those who curse you.[15]

If anyone forces you to go one mile, go with him two miles.[16]

If anyone slaps you on the right cheek, turn to him the other also.[17]

None of those things come *naturally*. They're as counterintuitive as kissing the wave.

A few days after his denial, Peter informed his friends, "I'm going out to fish."[18] This seems innocent enough, but it's more than a statement of fact. It's a declaration of intent. What did Peter do before becoming a disciple? He was a professional fisherman. I think Peter was going back to his old way of life, which is what we tend to do when we make mistakes. We throw in the towel. That's how mistakes become losing streaks. We flip the script the wrong way!

The next morning, Jesus showed up on the shoreline. Peter and his crew hadn't caught anything all night; then they heard someone say, "Try the other side!" The other side of the boat was only seven and a half feet away! Come on—do you really think the fish were hiding on the other side of the boat? The disciples flipped sides, and Jesus flipped the script. They caught so many fish that Peter immediately knew who the Monday Morning Fisherman was. He jumped out of the boat, fully clothed, and swam to shore. You gotta love this guy!

Your miracle may be closer than you think! It may be only seven and a half feet away. The question is this: Are you willing to try the other side? It's the little steps of obedience that often take the most faith!

FULL-CIRCLE MOMENT

After they hauled the miraculous catch of fish to shore, Jesus made the disciples breakfast on the beach. Then He asked Peter a pointed question: "Do you love me?"[19] He asked the question three times. The third time, Peter was *grieved*. This was no coincidence. This was genius. It was a full-circle moment.

Is it possible that Jesus knew something about reconditioned reflexes long before Ivan Pavlov came along? Peter denied Jesus three times. What did Jesus do? He restored Peter not once, not twice, but thrice! This was Jesus connecting the dots for Peter.

Sometimes you have to hurt someone to help him or her. That's a dangerous thing to write because lots of people do it the wrong way for the wrong reasons. Speak the truth in love, not because you have something to get off your chest. There is nothing easy about tough love. It's kissing the wave by asking the tough questions, having the hard conversations. It's caring enough to confront what's wrong because you have someone's best interests at heart.

Have you ever noticed when this recommissioning took place? John's gospel is explicit: "At dawn."[20] When do roosters crow? This was not coincidence; this was providence. This was Jesus reconditioning Peter's reflexes in a way he would never forget. The sound of a rooster's crow, which once triggered guilt, became a daily reminder of God's amazing grace!

With one act of grace, Peter postimagined his past.

With one act of grace, God flipped the script.

With one act of grace, a new chapter began.

Unleashing the power of twenty-four hours starts at the foot of the cross of Christ. You mean the cross to Christ. His hands and feet were punctured with nine-inch nails so you could overcome the pain of the past. His victory over sin and death was once for all, but it must be experienced every day. The good news? "His mercies . . . are new every morning."[21]

It's time to turn the page on the past. We've buried dead yesterdays by flipping the script and kissing the wave. It's time to win the day.

PART TWO

Win the Day

There are days, and then there are days that change every day thereafter. Of course, those life-altering days usually start like every other day! When the apostles woke up on the Day of Pentecost, they had no idea what was about to happen. What seemed like an ordinary day would become the *birthday* of the church. You cannot *plan* Pentecost, but you can *prepare* for it. How? By praying in an upper room for ten days in a row![1] If you do the right thing day in and day out, you will eventually unleash the power of twenty-four hours.

There is a scene in the film *Stranger than Fiction* that ranks as one of my all-time favorites. It's full of hope—in a quirky sort of way. The following quotation is a synopsis of Harold Crick's entire life, a life of absolute predictability:

> *Every weekday, for twelve years, Harold would brush each of his thirty-two teeth seventy-six times. Thirty-eight times back and forth. Thirty-eight times up and down.*[2]

Harold Crick's dental hygienist must have *loved* him! So did his boss. As a senior auditor for the IRS, Harold averaged 7.134 tax returns every day for twelve years. He took a 45.7-minute lunch break every day, along with a 4.3-minute coffee break. I'm an advocate of daily rituals, as you're about to discover, but that borders on obsessive compulsive!

Harold's life was governed by his wristwatch until one fateful day when he missed the bus for the first time in twelve years. "This was an extraordinary day," announced the film's narrator. "A day to be remembered for the rest of Harold's life." I love this next line: "Harold just thought it was a Wednesday."

One reason I love this scene in *Stranger than Fiction* is that it's not fictitious. Not to me, anyway. It reminds me of an otherwise-ordinary Wednesday in the summer of 2009 when I got a phone call that would change the trajectory of National Community Church. Like Harold, I just thought it was a Wednesday! The caller told me that he and his wife wanted to make a $3 million investment in our church. At the time, that gift exceeded the church's entire annual income!

I'll never forget what he said next: "We're giving this gift because you have vision beyond your resources." While we're on the subject, don't let your budget determine your vision. Why? God's vision for you is bigger than yours. Plus, He owns "the cattle on a thousand hills."[3] By definition, a God-sized dream is beyond your ability and beyond your resources. You can't make it a reality, but God can. In fact, God can do more in a single day than you can accomplish in a thousand lifetimes!

In part 2, we turn the page on the past and unleash the power of twenty-four hours. Two habits will help you make the most of every day, even the bad days. You've got to *eat the frog* and *fly the kite*. I'll define those habits, and we'll unpack them in practical ways. But winning the day starts with a mindset.

My self-confidence is subpar, but my holy confidence is off the charts. Why? Because I believe in the cumulative effect of long obedience in the same direction. If you do the right thing day in and day out, God is going to show up and show off. I've seen it too many times not to believe it. It won't be on our terms or our timeline—that's for sure! But if you do little things like they're big things, God will do big things like they're little things!

> Consecrate yourselves, for tomorrow the LORD will do
> amazing things among you.[4]

We want to do amazing things for God, but that isn't our job. God is the one who does amazing things for us and through us! Our job is to consecrate ourselves to God every day. If you win the day, amazing is on the way. You take care of today, and tomorrow is God's end of the bargain.

Habit 3—Eat the Frog

If you want God to do the super,
you've got to do the natural.

If you ever have to eat a live frog, it's best done first thing in the morning. Mark Twain is purported to have given this advice.[1] If you have to eat two frogs, he reportedly recommended eating the bigger one first. I know this scenario is awfully unlikely, but it's good advice nonetheless. Why eat the live frog first thing in the morning, you ask? Because you can go through the rest of your day knowing that the hardest task is behind you!

What to-do list items are you most tempted to procrastinate on? What goals have you had forever but not taken the first step toward? What difficult decision have you been delaying? That, my friend, is your frog! Give yourself a deadline; then get started. That is the third habit, and it's a hard one to swallow. Sorry—couldn't resist.

The bottom line? You can't just pray like it depends on God. You also have to work like it depends on you. If you want God to do the *super,* you've got to do the *natural.* And you have to start first thing in the morning.

How you start the day sets the tone for the rest of it, yet many of us never give the morning a second thought beyond getting out the door on time. Our morning rituals are as unplanned as an earthquake. Is that the best way to start the day? Que será será—whatever will be will be.

That's sounding the retreat before the day even begins. If you want to win the day, you've got to attack the day. How? Eat the frog.

Some people like to ease into the day without breaking a sweat, and I totally get that. Perhaps even sleep in on occasion, which is totally fine. But there is something to be said for starting the day with a challenge. It might be raising your heart rate via exercise or lowering your blood pressure via meditation. Either way, consistency is king. Consistency beats intensity seven days a week!

I had a father-in-law who placed a high priority on prayer. After his treadmill workout at four o'clock, he was kneeling in prayer by five o'clock. He read three newspapers every morning and attempted at least one crossword puzzle. He did all that before most people wake up! Of course, he grew up on a farm, which seems like an unfair advantage. He was used to milking the cows, which is not unlike eating the frog. Three newspapers and a crossword puzzle before breakfast may not be your thing, and that's okay. The question is, *What is your thing?*

I have a friend who doesn't get out of bed in the morning without going through a series of mental exercises. I don't know about you, but I'd fall back asleep! Plus, the bathroom is calling my name. Somehow my friend finds a way to focus. He flexes his gratitude muscle, giving thanks. Then he stretches his faith, praying for the people he loves. Early-morning meditation may not be your thing, especially if you're prone to hit the snooze button. The question is, *What is your thing?*

My sister-in-law Nicole Schmidgall starts the day with an intense boot camp—before sunrise! Sounds like fun, doesn't it? Somehow she completed 250 workouts this past year and has the certificate to prove it. Boot camp may not be your thing, and that's okay. But you know what question is coming: *What is your thing?*

What's the one thing you least like to do but you feel best about afterward? That's your frog. It's often the hardest habit to establish, but it pays the biggest dividends. Whatever it is, you've got to figure out a morning routine that works for you. And, I might add, one that works for your spouse and your kids and your dog and your boss. You don't have to shirk your responsibilities to eat the frog. All you have to do is plan your work, then work your plan. The good news? Well-begun is half-done! If you do the natural, it sets God up to do something super.

It's time to eat the frog!

5

Habit Stacking

You don't find time; you make time.

On May 17, 2014, Admiral William H. McRaven delivered the commencement address at his alma mater, the University of Texas at Austin. His advice to those graduating Longhorns? "If you want to change the world, start off by making your bed." That doesn't sound like life-altering advice, but daily habits yield compound interest over time. Starting off your day by making your bed is similar to William Osler's advice of living in day-tight compartments.

Admiral McRaven's military career ended when he was the ninth commander of the United States Special Operations Command, but much of his thirty-seven-year career was spent as a Navy SEAL officer. McRaven turned his speech into a *New York Times* bestseller, sharing the lessons that Navy SEAL training had taught him about life. The first lesson?

Start your day with a completed task.[1]

Before going any further, let me put your mind at ease. I'm not going to go Marky Mark on you. Mark Wahlberg, one of Hollywood's highest-paid actors, is infamous for his early-morning routine that begins with a wake-up call at two thirty. Yes, in the morning! Benjamin Franklin said, "Early to bed and early to rise makes a man healthy, wealthy, and wise." But that's ridiculous! If you're a night owl, you haven't even hit your first REM cycle!

Mark Wahlberg starts his morning routine with prayer and ends with cryotherapy, which is fantastic. He has two workouts, two showers, and two breakfasts. Good for him. Oh, I almost forgot. He picks up his kids from school before his afternoon workout. He does all this while making blockbuster movies! If you can pull that off, more power to you. But you'd better go to bed when Wahlberg does—seven thirty. Yes, in the evening!

I'm a student of and a proponent of daily rituals, but a reality check is in order. There are days when simply getting out of bed is winning the day. Don't be discouraged by the seemingly superhuman schedules of the superfamous! You are not Marky Mark, and that's okay. You be you. You do you. And remember, daily rituals were made to be broken. They rarely work like clockwork, especially if you have young children. Or a dog. Or a job. Or a cold. Or a commute. Or a life. That said, whether you get up at two thirty or ten thirty, make the bed.

CATCH A CAB

Twyla Tharp is one of the most accomplished choreographers of the modern era. Her credits include 129 dance compositions, twelve television specials, six Hollywood films, four Broadway shows, two figure-skating routines, and a partridge in a pear tree. All right, no partridge. But Twyla Tharp has won two Emmys, one Tony, and the prestigious Kennedy Center Honor. Did I mention her nineteen, count them, nineteen honorary doctorates?[2]

How has Twyla Tharp produced such an impressive LinkedIn profile? You guessed it—one day at a time! "I begin each day of my life with a ritual," said Twyla. "The quasi-religious power I attach to this ritual keeps me from rolling over and going back to sleep."[3] What is her ritual? After waking up at five thirty, she puts on her workout clothes, walks out of her Manhattan home, and hails a cab to take her to the Pumping Iron Gym at Ninety-First Street and First Avenue. "The ritual is not the stretching and weight training I put my body through each morning at the gym," said Twyla. "The ritual is the cab."[4] We'll come back to the cab because it's an important cue when it comes to habit stacking.

Does Twyla enjoy her two-hour workout every day? Her answer is no different from yours. There are days when she doesn't feel like going to the gym, but she doesn't give herself an out. That is the genius of eat-the-frog rituals. They eliminate excuses. More specifically, they eliminate the option of opting out. You can't wait until your alarm goes off to decide whether to work out. We all know how that story ends—with the snooze button! The decision has to be made beforehand, with a predecision. Then that predecision has to be put into deliberate practice with a well-designed ritual. That brings us back to the cab and the role it plays in Twyla's ritual.

> It's a simple act, but doing it the same way each morning habitualizes it—makes it repeatable, easy to do. It reduces the chance that I would skip it or do it differently. It is one more item in my arsenal of routines, and one less thing to think about.[5]

Ritualization gets a bit of a bad rap, and there can definitely be a downside to the things we do repeatedly. It's easy to learn *how* and forget *why*. That's when we start going through the motions.

The key to sustained growth in any area of our lives is routine, but once the routine becomes routine, you have to reinvent the routine. It's called the law of requisite variety. If you don't disrupt the status quo, the law of diminishing returns kicks in. While recognizing the downside, we should acknowledge the upside to automating our actions through ritualization.

The blue jeans, black turtleneck, and New Balance shoes worn by Steve Jobs every day are exhibit A. Was Steve Jobs trying to make a fashion statement? I think not. So, why did he wear the same outfit every day? It was one less decision he had to make. It was one less thing he had to worry about. That's what daily rituals are all about. Along with maximizing our God-given potential, they also streamline our lives by saving time and energy. I'm not advocating the same outfit every day per se. But reducing the number of decisions we make every day buys back bandwidth for the big decisions.

MORNING ROUTINE

I always set my alarm to an even number. I always take my shoes off when I write. I won't even open a book if I don't have a pen to underline with. And as you already know, I double-check my side-view mirror after pumping gas to make sure I removed the pump. These are a few of my idiosyncrasies. I almost forgot—while eating brownies, I always put some on my front teeth and smile real big.

Just as we develop conditioned reflexes, we also acquire a repertoire of rituals through repetition. They may not be as extreme as Harold Crick brushing each of his thirty-two teeth seventy-six times, but all of us have rituals that become second nature. In one respect, this is good. If you want to win the day, you've got to identify the habits that have a high return on investment and ritualize them through well-designed routines. That said, you've got to reevaluate those routines with a degree of frequency.

When was the last time you did a comprehensive evaluation of your morning routine? When was the last time you adjusted your alarm clock to get up early and go after God with a little more intentionality? When was the last time you added to or subtracted from your morning routine because of a goal you're going after?

Ironically, the morning routine doesn't begin in the morning. It begins the night before, when you go to bed. There is a kind of genius to the Jewish clock. The Jewish day did not begin at the crack of dawn. It began at sundown. Notice the sequence of each creation day: "There was *evening*, and there was *morning*."[6] Ignoring this sequence is like ignoring the Sabbath. This ancient rhythm is counterclockwise, but it has the potential to revolutionize your life. If you want to win the day, you have to start at sundown.

Before I unpack more of my morning routine, let me try to reset our mindset. We take the rhythm of day and night for granted. It's all we've ever known. What if we saw it for what it really is, a gift from God? We get to start over every day! Each day is a new creation. There is a little death when we go to sleep and a little resurrection when we wake up.

READINESS SCORE

For my most recent birthday, Lora gave me a ring with infrared sensors that measure my heart rate, body temperature, and respiration rate. It gives me metrics on sleep cycles, including deep sleep. There is even a gyroscope that tracks movement. What can I say? My wife loves me! That ring introduced me to vital signs that I didn't even know were important. Did you know heart rate variability is a key component of rest and recovery? Me neither! Every day, my ring gives me a *readiness score* that is largely determined by how long and how well I slept the night before! My point? Your first task each day is getting a good night's sleep.

Are your sleep habits setting you up for success? That may not sound super spiritual, but good sleep is good stewardship! Let me share a few simple ideas to make your bedtime ritual more meaningful. Don't just count sheep; count blessings! When you go to sleep with a grateful heart, it enhances your REM cycles. "Do not let the sun go down on your anger."[7] For that matter, don't let the sun go down on pride or lust or unforgiveness either! Confession isn't just good for the soul; it's good for sleep. Finally, let prayer be your punctuation mark at the end of each day.

Your readiness for each new day is greatly influenced by bedtime rituals, but let me add some morning rituals to the mix. What time do you set your alarm for, and why? What is the first thing you do when you wake up? How do you wake up your kids? How do you leverage your morning coffee and your morning commute?

I know there are days when it's all you can do to get out of bed or get out the door. But within those hurried minutes, there are holy moments. Like time, you don't *find* them. You *make* them. Some of my earliest memories are my mom waking me up with a rousing rendition of the opening song from the musical *Oklahoma!*

Oh, what a beautiful morning!
Oh, what a beautiful day!
I've got a beautiful feeling—
Everything's going my way.[8]

If you want to win the day, get a small win right out of the gate. Do seven minutes of meditation. Read one chapter. Do your age in sit-ups. None of those things are time consuming. So, why don't we do them? Most goals are *important,* but they aren't *urgent.* Eating the frog is making time for the important things over and above the urgent things.

According to a survey, 81 percent of Americans want to write a book.[9] The number one obstacle preventing them from doing so? They can't find the time. And they never will. That's true of every goal. You don't *find* time to train for a marathon or get your graduate degree. You've got to *make* time.

My ring has taught me one more lesson: the most important things are the hardest things to measure. How do you measure love? How do you measure humility? How do you measure spiritual hunger? Or a sense of awe? Or joy unspeakable? Or the peace that passes understanding? To what degree are you trusting God's timing? Resting in God's grace?

Those spiritual vital signs are the hardest things to measure, yet nothing is more important.

ATTACK THE DAY

Few things test the limits of human endurance like Navy SEAL training. It includes ten-mile runs with fifty-pound backpacks and midnight swims in the freezing Pacific Ocean. The training develops tactical skills and survival skills that would make MacGyver proud. It's meant to push the limits of physical, emotional, and mental endurance. But every day begins the same way—with an exacting inspection of one's bed. In the words of Admiral McRaven,

> If you did it right, the corners would be square, the covers pulled tight, the pillow centered just under the headboard, and the extra blanket folded neatly at the foot of the rack.
>
> It was a simple task, mundane at best. But every morning we were required to make our bed to perfection. It seemed a little ridiculous at the time, particularly in light of the fact that we were aspiring to be real warriors, tough battle-hardened SEALs, but the wisdom of this simple act has been proven to me many times over.
>
> If you make your bed every morning, you will have accomplished the first task of the day.[10]

There are countless things you cannot control every day. The dog leaves a good-morning gift next to your bed. Your children's hair doesn't cooperate with your comb. Neither does their attitude. A traffic jam kills your commute time, which affects the rest of the day. Some days start off wrong, and no matter how hard you try, you can't seem to course correct. But even on those days that spin out of control, we are still response-able.

For all the things we cannot control, we have the Serenity Prayer. But along with praying like it depends on God, we have to work like it depends on us. Generally speaking, we can control when we get up. We can control when we go to bed. And we can control our attitude in between! Don't let what you cannot control keep you from controlling what you can.

My morning routine starts with a hot shower. I know cold showers have health benefits, not to mention a cult following. I've done a personal cost-benefit analysis, and the answer is "No, thank you!" I take a hot shower, and water pressure is key. Have you ever stayed at a hotel where the water dribbles out of the showerhead? Tough way to start the day!

After showering, I eat a light breakfast. I did not do this for about a decade, and I paid the price in pounds. Despite eating less, I put on twenty-five pounds. No, it was not muscle. My affinity for caramel macchiatos may have factored into my weight gain. I was running on empty and didn't realize it. Actually, I was running on caffeine and sugar.

How did that change? I complained about fatigue to the life coach who did my life plan. On the first day of that retreat, he made an observation: "Mark, I noticed that you got up very early. You didn't eat breakfast. We did several hours of intense mental exercises. Then you went for a run. All of that before eating. Could that be causing your lack of energy?" We all need a Captain Obvious in our lives.

It's amazing how ignorant we can be when it comes to our own idiosyncrasies. We're robotic about rhythms and routines that are counterproductive. We don't deny GIGO—garbage in, garbage out—but we don't eat like it's true. Why? Because each of us thinks we're the exception to the rule. That's our rule of life.

The bottom line? We all have blind spots that don't allow us to see what is hidden in plain sight. It's those blind spots that allow us to continue in bad habits without giving them a second thought. This is where a coach or pastor or mentor is critical. Or a good friend who cares enough—and is courageous enough—to say what everyone else sees!

GOD TIME

Just as there are days that change every day thereafter, the same is true of books! For me, one of those life-changing books is *Lessons from the*

Life of Moody. Not unlike the twenty-two words that altered William Osler's life, one providential paragraph altered mine. It inspired a discipline that I've put into practice for more than two decades. It's the most important part of my morning routine by far.

> Every day of his life, I have reason for believing, he arose very early in the morning to study the Word of God, way down to the close of his life. Mr. Moody used to rise about four o'clock in the morning to study the Bible. He would say to me: "If I am going to get in any study, I have got to get up before the other folks get up," and he would shut himself up in a remote room in his house, alone with his God and his Bible.[11]

I underlined that paragraph twenty-five years ago, and it has underscored my life ever since. Have I always succeeded at practicing spiritual disciplines as part of my early-morning routine? Not even close! I've had many false starts. And for the record, I'm not up at four o'clock in the morning. But when I'm hitting on all cylinders, it's because I got in some good God time.

"Your first ritual that you do during the day is the highest leveraged ritual, by far," said Eben Pagan, "because it has the effect of setting your mind, and setting the context, for the rest of your day."[12] A really good morning ritual is like Archimedes's lever; it can move heaven and earth.

At this point, I'd better acknowledge that some people accomplish their goals by staying up a little later at night. To each his own! You've got to figure out what works for you. My day usually begins by six o'clock in the morning, unless it's my writing season. From Thanksgiving until Super Bowl Sunday, I'm up and at it a little earlier than that. I also get to bed a little earlier, except for Monday Night Football. All right, Thursday Night Football too. Okay, Sunday Night Football as well. But every other night, I get to bed earlier! And I do compensate with a nap the next day!

Speaking of naps, I'm a huge fan. According to research done by NASA, a twenty-six-minute nap improves job performance by 34 percent and alertness by up to 54 percent.[13] I don't just love that study; I live it. I can't verify this, but I'm convinced that 90 percent of my creativity happens before noon. When my circadian rhythm dips in early afternoon, so does my creativity. If I'm able to catch a quick nap, it resets my mind and opens a second window of creativity.

I'm not sure which way you're wired—morning person or night owl. Either way, you have to attack the day. Whether you get up before or after the sun rises, you still need to eat the frog sooner rather than later.

HABIT STACKING

During my God time, I read Scripture while drinking a cup of coffee. Actually, it's a small latte with two shots of espresso. Remember Twyla Tharp? That latte is my cab. The technical term is *habit stacking*. It's coupling a habit that comes easy, like drinking coffee, with a habit that requires a little more discipline.

When your office is right above the coffeehouse you own and operate, coffee is like clockwork. You don't start your day any other way. Why would you? In fact, you have to tell the baristas to cut you off when you've had a few too many shots of espresso!

While we're on the subject of coffee, Ludwig van Beethoven began his day at dawn with a carefully crafted cup of coffee. Long before coffee scales and French presses, Beethoven would count sixty coffee beans, one at a time, for the perfect brew. Then there is Teddy Roosevelt, who purportedly drank a gallon of coffee every day. His son likened his coffee cup to a bathtub, which might explain his boundless energy. Did you know that he holds the record for the most handshakes in a single day? I'm not sure who was counting, but he managed to shake 8,150 hands in one day![14]

I'm not recommending a gallon of coffee per day, but I do have a little formula that I came up with many years ago: *The Holy Spirit + Caffeine = Awesome!* The same could be said of Holy Scripture. A caffeinated drink makes the Bible taste even better.

I wish good habits came as easy as bad habits, but they do not. That's why I piggyback harder habits on ones that come more naturally, like coffee. When I start sipping my latte, I start reading my Bible. By the time I'm done with that cup of coffee, I've caffeinated my soul. It makes both habits more enjoyable.

Habit stacking is designing daily rituals by leveraging everyday activities. If you pray before meals, you're already habit stacking! When you get out of bed or go to bed, why not hit your knees in prayer? You're already halfway there! When you go to the bathroom, fill up your water bottle. When you get home from work, kiss your spouse and hug your kids. Habit stacking is not rocket science! All it requires is intentionality coupled with consistency.

After I wrote *Draw the Circle,* our church did its first forty-day prayer challenge. We've done it many times since then, including during the COVID-19 crisis. We leverage 7:14 a.m. as a prayer alarm, hitting our knees in prayer no matter where we are. Why 7:14? We're kneeling on the promise in 2 Chronicles 7:14: "If my people, who are called by my name, will humble themselves and pray and seek my face and turn from their wicked ways, then I will hear from heaven, and I will forgive their sin and will heal their land." We've turned that time into a trigger. We've turned that verse into an alarm. You can do the same thing with different times, different places. It's a creative way of habit stacking.

RITUAL REMINDERS

The idea of ritualizing everyday activities is as old as the Jewish people putting ritual reminders called mezuzah on their doorframes. Instead of compartmentalizing the commandments, they integrated them into their daily routines. How? Through the mother of all learning—repetition. "Repeat them again and again to your children."[15]

This sounds like rote learning, but it required creativity and intentionality. It involved environmental engineering and choice architecture. They surrounded themselves with ritual reminders that sacramentalized every moment.

Did you know that an observant Jewish person pronounces a hundred blessings a day? If you do something a hundred times a day, it becomes a way of life! That may seem impossible, unattainable. But that is where habit stacking comes into play. You've got to leverage chronology and geography. "Talk about them when you sit at home and when you walk along the road, when you lie down and when you get up."[16]

If you want to start habit stacking, this is a great place to start. Leverage the first few minutes and last few minutes of the day—"when you lie down and when you get up." Find creative ways to ritualize your work. For me, it's taking off my shoes while I write. And make sure you add your commute to the mix! The average commute time in America is twenty-six minutes one way![17] That equates to lots of audiobooks or podcasts or prayer.

Can I challenge you to try a little experiment? Put a book in your bathroom! If you habit stack your bathroom time with a good book, you can read a book a month. And some of you have more potential than that. It's a better use of bathroom time than scrolling your social media feeds! Yes, I'm having a little bit of fun. But I want to bring this idea down to earth.

When I felt called to write, I started reading about two hundred books a year. Many people find that hard to believe, but I was pastoring nineteen people our first year! I had some time on my hands. But I didn't just *find* time; I *made* time. We didn't have smartphones or social media. That alone adds hours back into the day! What inspired me? I heard that the average author puts about two years of life experience into a book. At twenty-five, life experience is what I was lacking! I did the math. If I read two hundred books in a year, I'd gain four hundred years of life experience. When people ask me how old I am, I often answer in book years. I'm at least seven thousand years old.

Hang a Harp

There is an old idiom that traces all the way back to Aristotle: "Well-begun is half-done." Morning rituals are like the daily double in *Jeopardy!* Not only do they set the tone for the rest of the day; they also pay dividends all day long! That said, momentum is either gained or lost throughout the day.

How do you build on those morning rituals?

How do you gain momentum as the day goes on?

How do you shift momentum if your day got off to a bad start?

Too many Christians become *less* like Christ as the day wears on. The day takes its toll, turning us into trolls by the time we get home from work. Dr. Jekyll turns into Mr. Hyde. What makes righteous people different? One factor is emotional fortitude, and I would couple it with emotional intelligence. Their fuses are a little longer. "All day long," said the psalmist, "they are merciful and deal graciously."[18]

There is a medieval monastic practice called the daily office that divides the day into a liturgy of the hours. You've probably heard of a few of these prayer times, like evening vespers and midnight vigils.

The idea of the daily office is often traced back to a brilliant book written in AD 516, *The Rule of Saint Benedict*. Benedict divided the day into eight prayer periods, but his rule of life was patterned after a more ancient rhythm. The daily office dates all the way back to King David, who said, "I will praise you seven times a day."[19]

According to rabbinic tradition, David hung his harp over his bed by an open window. It functioned as an ancient alarm clock. When the north winds started blowing, the sound of the strings would wake him up, and he would study the Torah until the break of dawn. "Awake, harp and lyre!" he said. "I will awaken the dawn."[20]

I realize that praying seven times a day may sound otherworldly, especially if you have fussy children, leaky faucets, and bills to pay. Daniel's daily office may be a little more attainable than David's. Daniel knelt three times a day and prayed in his upstairs bedroom.[21]

If you start the day and end the day with prayer, all you have to do is add one more prayer time to the mix. There is no better way— no other way—to sustain spiritual momentum.

There is nothing wrong with sleeping in now and then, but you've got to hang a harp like David did. You've got to find a place to turn into an altar like Daniel did. There is nothing wrong with talk radio, but could your commute time be leveraged more effectively? You've got to figure out what works for you, then give it a go. And like everything else we attempt for the first time, there will be some trial and error! Don't throw in the towel if you miss a day. All of us do.

CURSE THE BARREN FIG TREE

Still feel like you can't *find* the time? Me neither! You've got to *make* time.

Eating the frog isn't easy. It's choosing the *important* over the *urgent*. It's figuring out your high-leverage habits, then investing your time and talent in them. It's recognizing your unique gift to the world and utilizing it. It's recognizing that time can be spent only once so it must be spent wisely. Saying yes to one thing is saying no to something else!

Here are a few tips, a few tricks that have helped me eat the frog.

First, *curse the barren fig tree.*

Eating the frog involves analyzing your time. Remember when Jesus cursed the barren fig tree? Why did He curse it? Because it wasn't bearing any fruit.[22] You've got to curse the barren fig trees—those bad habits that waste time, talent, and treasure. A *stop-doing list* is a good place to start. Then you've got to identify the good habits that net the highest return on investment. Those are the things you can't afford *not* to do!

Second, *do the math.*

When I'm in a writing season, I try to get off the grid. It's not easy saying no to meeting requests during that season, but there is no other way to hit a deadline. The way I see it, books are my way of spending five hours with anybody, anywhere, anytime. I eat the frog by blocking off writing days on my calendar. Even then, it's not easy saying no. To help ease my conscience, I do the math. There is tremendous value in meeting with someone one on one, but my time is multiplied only by a factor of one. With books, my time is multiplied by the total number of readers. My bestselling book, *The Circle Maker,* equates to 1,141 years of reading time at last count. I don't want to waste anyone's time by writing a book that is less than my best. Doing the math helps me protect my writing time because writing is my high-leverage habit.

Third, *establish healthy boundaries.*

During a recent building project, I made a predecision to limit my overnight speaking trips to seven nights per year. That meant saying no to lots of opportunities, but I wanted to prioritize my family. This decision saved my sanity during a stressful season. If you have a hard time saying no, like me, have someone else say it for you. This may be tipping my cards, but many years ago, I asked our stewardship team to limit the number of boards I could serve on simultaneously. Why? Because I know myself. I have a tendency to stretch myself too thin. I've never encountered an opportunity that didn't seem like an *amazing* opportunity! Healthy boundaries keep my people-pleasing propensities in check. All right, my ego too!

While we're on the subject of boundaries, do you keep a Sabbath? If you think the world revolves around you, it's awfully hard to take a day off. You're afraid of falling behind. We become like the Red Queen in *Through the Looking-Glass,* who yelled, "Faster! Faster!" If that doesn't describe our pace of life, I'm not sure what does! "It takes all the running *you* can do, to keep in the same place. If you want to get somewhere else, you must run at least twice as fast as that!"[23] We suffer from "hurry sickness"! It's this feeling of anxious urgency. We feel like we're chronically short on time, and we get flustered by every delay.[24] A Sabbath is the only solution. It's a weekly reminder that the world doesn't revolve around us! God can keep the planets in orbit without your help, thank you very much!

Put It on the Calendar

What frog do you need to eat?

What are you waiting for?

If you don't define *when* and *where* you will eat the frog, it will never happen. A dream without a deadline is called a wish. You've got to put it on the calendar! The way you make time is by scheduling your top priorities first, then letting things of lesser importance fall off your to-do list.

Let me take a page out of Eugene Peterson's datebook. As a writer and a pastor, Eugene hit a point where the demands of his dual-calling were unsustainable, so he scheduled a two-hour meeting with "FD" three afternoons a week. Who was this mysterious FD? None other than Fyodor Dostoevsky. No, they were not contemporaries! Eugene couldn't find a living mentor, so he chose a dead one. He managed to read through Dostoevsky's entire corpus in seven months! "Then the crisis was over," said Eugene. "Thanks to Dostoevsky, God and passion would never again be at risk."[25]

The Catholic priest and professor Henri Nouwen took even more drastic measures. He once spent seven months in a Trappist monastery. Why? He had done so much lecturing on prayer that he didn't have time to pray. "I started to see how much I had indeed fallen in love with my own compulsions and illusions, and how much I needed to step back," he said. Then he asked himself a brave question: "Is there a quiet stream underneath the fluctuating affirmations and rejections of my little world? Is there a still point where my life is anchored and from which I can reach out with hope and courage and confidence?"[26]

Is there a quiet stream?

Is there a still point where your life is anchored?

What habit will yield the highest return? How can you make it part of your daily routine? The key, no matter what it is, is identifying *when* and *where*. Let me present one more piece of evidence; then I'll close this case.

In the 1960s, a study was done involving students at Yale University. Graduating seniors were educated about the dangers of tetanus and given the opportunity to get a free inoculation at the health center. Despite the fact that it was free and the majority of the students were convinced they needed to get the shot, only 3 percent followed through and got the vaccine. Why? Well, if you don't define *when* and *where,* you have a 3 percent chance of success!

There was another group of graduating seniors, the test group, that was given the same lecture with one caveat. They were given copies of the campus map with the location of the health center circled. So they knew *where.* Then they were asked to look at their weekly schedule and figure out *when* they would get the shot. Nine times as many students in this group got inoculated.[27] Good intentions are good, but they aren't good enough. You've got to map it. You've got to put it on the calendar! What then? Eat the frog!

The Mundanity of Excellence

Slow and steady wins the race.

How long do you think you can hold your breath? A minute? Maybe two? Let's have a little fun at the beginning of this chapter and find out. Go ahead—give it a try. If you make it more than thirty seconds, you're actually above average. Given our little experiment, can you imagine holding your breath for seventeen minutes and four seconds? Impossible, right? Yet that's what David Blaine did on the set of *The Oprah Winfrey Show* on April 30, 2008.

David Blaine has pulled off some unbelievable stunts. He endured a million volts of electricity for seventy-three hours while standing atop a twenty-two-foot pillar.[1] He was buried alive for seven days in a clear coffin. He went without food for forty-four days while encased in a plastic box that was suspended by a crane. He caught a .22-caliber bullet in his mouth. He also regurgitated live frogs.[2] Take that, Mark Twain! Few magicians are more accomplished than David Blaine, but David Blaine doesn't even believe in magic! Yes, you read that right.

Before we go any further, let me back up just a little bit. In 1987, Blaine heard about a boy who fell through ice and was trapped underwater for forty-five minutes. Hypoxic brain damage usually sets in at six minutes, but when rescue workers resuscitated the boy, there was no brain damage. It might not qualify as a signature story for Blaine, but it incited a subplot. He noted that the boy's body temperature had dropped to seventy-seven degrees. "As a magician, I think everything is possible," said Blaine. "If something is done by one person, it can be done by others."

He began talking with experts about respiration. A doctor friend said, "David, you're a magician, create the illusion of not breathing, it will be much easier." Blaine toyed with different ways of breaking the breath-holding record, including a lung bypass machine. He landed on the craziest idea of all—actually doing it. At the outset, he was absolutely average. His first attempt to hold his breath lasted less than a minute, but he isn't easily deterred.

Every morning for many months, Blaine would begin the day by holding his breath for forty-four out of the first fifty-two minutes of the day, with brief breaths interspersed. The oxygen deprivation caused awful headaches, but he kept pushing his limits day after day. He lost fifty pounds in three months to increase lung capacity. Finally, David Blaine was ready to attempt the world record on national television, but he made one critical mistake. Television producers thought that holding his breath would be boring, so they had him handcuffed underwater. The extra movement wasted oxygen, and Blaine blacked out before having to be rescued.

"I had failed on every level," he said. "So, naturally, the only way out of the slump that I could think of was, I decided to call Oprah." I'm sure you have her on speed dial too! David Blaine held his breath for a record-breaking seventeen minutes and four seconds, with Oprah Winfrey watching![3]

THE CULT OF GENIUS

"In the case of everything perfect we are accustomed to abstain from asking how it became," said the German philosopher Friedrich Nietzsche. "We rejoice in the present fact as though it came out of the ground by magic."[4] This idea that a select few have seeming superpowers while the rest of us schlep our way through life is what Nietzsche called "the cult of genius."[5] Only those with extraordinary innate talent are inducted. That excludes just about everyone, including William Osler, Bo Eason, Elon Musk, Twyla Tharp, and David Blaine. My guess is that you can add your name to that list as well.

Truth be told, the cult of genius is a little like the Wizard of Oz. If you peek behind the curtain, you find ordinary people a lot like you—lions who lack courage, scarecrows who lack intelligence, and tin men who lack heart. I'm not ignoring the fact that there are child prodigies who skew the bell curve, but no one comes out of the womb walking!

Remember our original hypothesis? *Almost anybody can accomplish almost anything if they work at it long enough, hard enough, and smart enough.* It doesn't just happen—poof. It'll involve some early mornings and some late nights. It'll involve some blood, sweat, and tears. The good news? If you do the natural, it sets God up to do something super. Miracles happen at the place where our grit meets God's grace.

In her groundbreaking book on grit, Angela Duckworth pushed Nietzsche's envelope: "Mythologizing natural talent lets us all off the hook." How? We excuse the success that others achieve as the confluence of factors they could not control and we cannot replicate. Simply put, they won the talent lottery. That, of course, allows the rest of us to maintain the status quo. "We prefer our excellence fully formed," said Duckworth. "We prefer mystery to mundanity."[6]

On that note, let me double back to David Blaine. His TED Talk, "How I Held My Breath for 17 Minutes," has been watched twenty-six million times. At the end of that talk, Blaine revealed the secret behind his magic. If you were expecting something magical, it's a little bit of a letdown.

As a magician, I try to show things to people that seem impossible. And I think magic, whether I'm holding my breath or shuffling a deck of cards, is pretty simple. It's practice, it's training, and it's—

That's when David Blaine started crying on stage. And no, it wasn't an act. Then he regained his composure and picked up where he left off.

> It's practice, it's training and experimenting, while pushing through the pain to be the best that I can be. And that's what magic is to me.[7]

If I'm hearing him right, magic is anything but magic. Correct me if I'm wrong, but that sounds a lot like deliberate practice, doesn't it? Magic is outworking everyone else. Or you can flip that coin and pull it out from behind your ear. Working longer, harder, and smarter makes magic. Either way, there is no abracadabra. The only hocus-pocus is practicing like George "the Shotgun" Shuba, training like Twyla Tharp, and experimenting like David Blaine. What do they have in common? They all chose to eat the frog every day. Of course, David Blaine eats the frog literally and metaphorically!

EXCELLENCE IS MUNDANE

More than three decades ago, sociologist Daniel Chambliss initiated a study of Olympic swimmers with the goal of identifying least common denominators that led to their success. That study, "The Mundanity of Excellence," was groundbreaking in more ways than one. It married sports and sociology while demystifying the idea of excellence. Chambliss didn't deny the role that genetics plays in the pool, but he was unapologetic in his assessment. Simply put, " 'talent' does not lead to excellence."[8] Contrary to popular opinion, it never has. And it never will.

Michael Phelps is the most decorated Olympian of all time, winner of twenty-three gold medals. His six-foot, seven-inch wingspan and size fourteen flippers don't hurt—that's for sure! Anatomically speaking, his torso is freakishly long, while his lower body is surprisingly short. It's like he's tailor made for the pool, but we tend to overemphasize genetics while underappreciating work ethic.

When Phelps was a teenager, his coach asked whether he'd be willing to work out on Sundays. Michael agreed, and his coach said, "Great. We just got 52 more workouts in than your competitors, because most people take Sundays off."[9]

I'd better add a sidebar right here. There is a point of diminishing return when *more is less* and *less is more*! Elite athletes rest and recover with the same intentionality as they work out. Even God took a day off. It's called the Sabbath. If you want to be at the top of your game, whatever game that is, observe the Sabbath and keep it holy![10] Besides, all work and no play makes Jack a dull boy!

That said, the gold medal generally goes to the person who puts in the most time and effort. All other things being equal, fifty-two extra workouts is what wins the gold, wins the day. And that's true no matter what you do. The secret is surprisingly simple: "Excellence is mundane."[11] I know—makes you want to slam this book shut. Maybe even toss it across the room. But you know it's true. I think this is actually good news for average Joes, average Janes. The playing field is more level than you may think.

It's easy to envy the success of others while ignoring the sacrifices that made it possible. Quit envying their outcomes and start imitating their inputs! Reverse engineer the people you respect. Can I let you in on a little secret? The more effortless something looks, the more effort went into it. Great musicians make hard look easy! Same with athletes. Pick a sport, any sport. When Phil Mickelson was a young golfer, he struggled with his short game. A coach challenged him to make one hundred three-foot putts in a row. After many attempts, Phil sunk ninety-nine in a row before missing his one hundredth attempt. Most of us would have rounded up! Not Phil Mickelson. He went right back at it until he accomplished the 100 Putt Challenge. That's how you win forty-four PGA events and five majors![12]

Through Chambliss's study, we learn that "excellence requires doing small, ordinary things consistently right."[13] Like three-foot putts! Excellence seems miraculous, but it's actually quite mundane. Excellence is a habit that is repeated consistently and correctly over and over again.

Few people exemplify excellence better than Horst Schulze, co-founder of the Ritz-Carlton Hotel Company. It was Horst who introduced the now-famous policy empowering Ritz-Carlton staff to spend up to $2,000 ensuring guest satisfaction. Horst got his start with a three-year internship at the Kurhaus hotel in Germany. His first job? Cleaning ashtrays. Upon proving himself, he graduated to washing dishes from seven in the morning until eleven at night. At the end of that sixteen-hour workday, Horst sometimes had to polish guests' shoes that had been left in the hallways.[14] Despite the long hours and mundane tasks, Horst Schulze fell in love with customer service.

This sounds a lot like making the bed, doesn't it? "If you can't do the little things right," observed Admiral McRaven, "you will never do the big things right."[15]

CONSISTENTLY CONSISTENT

We recently went through our annual review cycle at National Community Church, and I took note of one comment on one review of one employee. This employee may not be the most talented player on our team, but she was evaluated as "consistently consistent." I love the double emphasis. Again, consistency beats intensity seven days a week! It's hard to put a price tag on dependability, isn't it? Teachability too! I love people who show up on time, on task. I love people who refuse to make excuses. They make time to make it happen. They get it done, come hell or high water!

Speaking of water, do you know what Michael Phelps did after becoming the best in the world? He trained even harder, even longer—six hours a day, seven days a week, five years in a row! Do the math, and that's tough to beat. That's the point, and that's true of everything. If you want to be the best, you've got to log the hours. "If you'll spend one extra hour each day in the study of your chosen field," said Earl Nightingale, "you'll be a national expert in five years or less."[16]

The question, of course, is, How do you muster that kind of daily discipline? How do you keep on keeping on, even when you've reached the top rung of the ladder? Extrinsic motivation fades like marine layer fog. If you are motivated by extrinsic factors like fame or fortune, motivation eventually evaporates along with the accolades. Why? You're working for the wrong reasons!

Intrinsic motivation is the gift that keeps on giving. It's the thing that keeps us going after everybody else gets out of the pool. It's the thing that gets us up early and keeps us up late. Well, that and Red Bull.

What is intrinsic motivation? It's living for the applause of nail-scarred hands. It's giving God A-plus effort. It's recognizing that potential is God's gift to us and that what we do with it is our gift to God. It's not trying to be better than everybody else. It's trying to be better than you were yesterday!

ONE MORE LAP

Let me dive back into the pool one more time with one of the swimmers profiled by Daniel Chambliss. Compared with his compatriots, Rowdy Gaines got a late start at competitive swimming. He took up the sport at seventeen, but he made up for lost time with a grueling work ethic. Gaines won three gold medals at the 1984 Olympics, the year before Michael Phelps was born. He set eleven world records during his storied career. Here's where it gets good. Are you ready for this? Rowdy Gaines once calculated how many cumulative miles he had swum. Go ahead and venture a guess. Remember, Olympic-sized pools are only fifty meters long and Gaines was a sprinter. Got a guess?

Because America boycotted the Moscow Games in 1980, Rowdy spent eight years training for races that lasted less than one minute. That's worth repeating—*eight years for one minute*! Add up all the laps, and Gaines swam twenty thousand miles in fifty-meter increments! Or as he put it, "I swam around the world for a race that lasted forty-nine seconds."[17]

If that isn't the mundanity of excellence, I'm not sure what is. The mundanity of excellence is one more lap. It's choosing the pain of present-tense discipline over the pain of future-tense regret. That's the difference between good and great. And it's not true just in the Olympic pool; it's true in the kiddie pool.

In standardized math tests, Japanese children consistently score higher than their American counterparts. Some assume that a natural proclivity for mathematics is the primary difference—nature over nurture. But researchers have found that it may have more to do with effort than ability. In a study involving first graders, students were given a difficult puzzle to solve. The researchers weren't interested in whether the children could solve the puzzle. They wanted to see how long they would try before giving up.

The American children lasted, on average, 9.47 minutes. The Japanese children lasted 13.93 minutes. In other words, the Japanese children tried 47 percent longer. Is it any wonder that they scored higher on standardized math exams? Researchers concluded that the difference in math scores has less to do with intelligence quotient and more to do with persistence quotient. The Japanese first graders tried harder by trying longer.[18]

That study does more than explain the difference in standardized math scores. It doesn't matter whether it's athletics or academics, music or math. There are no shortcuts. There are no cheat codes. The only magic is outworking everyone else!

TRY, TRY AGAIN

The following proverb traces back to an educational reformer named Thomas Palmer:

If at first you don't succeed, try, try again.[19]

Sooner or later, persistence pays off. But let me add a twist or two. You can't just try longer. You have to try different, try smarter.

Two-thirds of smokers who want to quit never even try. Of those who do try, nine out of ten fail. And the one who does succeed, fails six times before succeeding.[20] The moral of the story? Keep trying! You know what's coming next: *almost anybody can accomplish almost anything if they work at it long enough, hard enough, and smart enough.* But I'd better add this addendum: succeeding may mean failing more than everyone else.

If you want to do what no one has *done,* you have to do what no one is *doing.* Sounds simple enough, but it takes tremendous courage. Do you know why Pixar started making movies? They couldn't sell enough copies of their animation software to make ends meet. Their business model wasn't working, so they tried something different. Aren't you glad they did?

What do you need to try different?

What do you need to try smarter?

Your system is perfectly designed for the results you're getting. If you don't like something, take response-ability for it. Then do something about it. Is there a dream that's gathering dust? A goal you've given up on? Try different. Try smarter. Try something.

Our first attempt at church planting failed, but we learned from it. Was it scary trying again? Absolutely. If you fail once, you can write it off as an anomaly. If you fail twice, it might be saying something about you. Part of eating the frog is swallowing your pride. It's giving God a second chance. Or you can flip that script—it's God giving you a second chance. Either way, you've got to try, try again. God hasn't given up on you; don't give up on God. Give it another go and see what He does.

What if the Israelites had quit circling the city of Jericho on day six? They would have missed out on the miracle by one day! You've got to keep circling. If you keep doing the natural, super will happen sooner or later.

FALSE POSITIVES

In 2009, the London Philharmonic Orchestra and its conductor, David Parry, selected and recorded what they believed to be the 50 greatest pieces of classical music. The list includes 5 pieces by Beethoven, 6 by Mozart, and 3 by Bach.[21] To create those masterpieces, Beethoven produced 650 pieces of music, Mozart wrote more than 600, and Bach composed more than 1,000.[22]

If they were baseball players, Mozart's batting average would have been .01—one in one hundred. You don't even make a Little League team with that kind of batting average. Bach's and Beethoven's batting averages were even worse! And Handel had only one hit.

There are two errors that we make in evaluation—a false positive and a false negative. A false positive is a false alarm. It's the boy who cried wolf when there was no wolf.[23] A false positive is believing something to be true that turns out to be false. In business, it's a product that is expected to be a home run but turns out to be a swing and a miss. I tried to start a business like that one time—GodiPod. It was a total wash.

A false negative is the opposite. It's expecting failure but experiencing success. When my publisher recommended that we turn *Chase the Lion* into a reading plan on YouVersion, I honestly thought it was a waste of time. It's been downloaded more than half a million times. Shows how much I know. That's why I write books instead of publishing them!

Let's double back to the fifty greatest compositions of all time. A psychologist named Aaron Kozbelt has examined letters written by Beethoven, in which he evaluated seventy of his works. Kozbelt compared Beethoven's self-assessment with the opinions of experts, and he found that Beethoven committed fifteen false positives. In other words, compositions that he thought were major turned out to be minor. He also committed eight false negatives. He criticized pieces that are some of his greatest works. That's a 33 percent error rate even after receiving audience feedback.[24]

I don't want to dumb down a well-researched study like the one just cited, but I feel like quoting a famous fish named Dory: "Just keep swimming."[25] Seems apropos given the study on Olympic swimmers. We overestimate what we can accomplish in a year or two, but we underestimate what God can do in ten or twenty years. It all comes back to eating the frog.

Remember Tim Ferriss and his two crappy pages a day? Or George Shuba and six hundred swings a day? Take the pressure of perfectionism off yourself. How? Keep writing music like Bach and Beethoven. Keep holding your breath like David Blaine. Keep swimming like Rowdy Gaines. Why? Slow and steady wins the race!

THE LITTLE ENGINE THAT COULD

On April 8, 1906, the *New-York Tribune* printed a sermon by Charles S. Wing that included a story about the little engine that could. The signature line, *I think I can,* became a common refrain in Sunday school classes across the country. The moral of the story? Doggedness wins the day! You just have to keep on keeping on.

I've written enough books and preached enough sermons to know that I don't know how they'll be received by God or by people. I have hunches, but they're often wrong. What do you do when you swing and miss? You keep getting back into the batter's box and swinging for the fences! Try different. Try longer. And if that doesn't work, try something else. Just keep trying!

Like me, I bet you've made your fair share of missteps and miscalculations. Winning the day isn't about getting it right *the first time.* It's about getting it right *eventually.* It's about getting back up no matter how many times you've fallen down. It's living to fight another day.

If you keep eating frogs, you'll eventually get there! Those two pages will eventually turn into a book. Those six hundred swings will eventually turn into a home run. Those 650 compositions will eventually turn into an all-time classic. Those twenty thousand miles of laps will eventually turn into a gold medal.

"People are always blaming their circumstances for what they are," said a character in one of George Bernard Shaw's plays. "I don't believe in circumstances." Me neither! "The people who get on in this world are the people who get up and look for the circumstances they want, and, if they can't find them, make them."[26]

The way you *make circumstances* is by *making time* for the habits that will create those circumstances. It's called the mundanity of excellence, and it's all about eating the frog. Well-begun is half-done—that's true. But the game never ends. You've got to keep swimming. Why? Slow and steady wins the race!

Habit 4—Fly the Kite

How you do anything
is how you'll do everything.

After their wedding in 1964, my parents drove halfway across the country to the Honeymoon Capital of the World. Niagara Falls consists of three waterfalls—the American Falls, Bridal Veil Falls, and Horseshoe Falls. They combine to produce the highest flow rate of any waterfall on earth—3,160 tons of water flowing over the falls every second and falling at a speed of thirty-two feet per second.[1] It's a beauty to behold, especially if you're honeymooning.

In the mid-eighteenth century, the only way to cross the Niagara Gorge was by boat. On November 9, 1847, a civil engineer named Charles Ellet Jr. was commissioned to build a suspension bridge across the chasm. Ellet naturally chose the narrowest neck, but it still presented an impossible challenge. How do you stretch the first wire across an 800-foot gorge with 225-foot cliffs on either side and rapids that rush toward a waterfall?

At dinner one night, Ellet's team brainstormed ways of getting that first cable across the chasm. One person proposed a rocket. Another suggested a cannon. That's when Theodore Graves Hulett came up with a rather ingenious idea—a cash prize for a kite flying contest. For the record, Hulett was full of offbeat ideas. He once cemented frogs into stone blocks, cut them open five years later, and discovered that their tissue was intact, a perfect cast of the frogs. That's when he altered his last will and testament, ordering the cementation of his own body upon death.[2] But I digress.

In January 1848, hundreds of kids tried flying kites across the gorge. If you know anything about weather conditions in that part of the country at that time of year, that's pretty impressive! A fifteen-year-old American named Homan Walsh took the ferry from the American side to the Canadian side to take advantage of the prevailing winds. He flew his kite all day, all night. When his kite string broke, he had to wait eight days to cross back over by ferry. He retrieved the kite, made repairs, and crossed over again. On January 30, 1848, Walsh's kite made it across the gorge, winning him the ten-dollar cash prize! The day following that successful flight, a stronger line was attached to the kite string and pulled across. Then an even stronger line. Then a rope. Then a cable consisting of thirty-six strands of ten-gauge wire.[3]

The *Buffalo Daily Courier* published this account on January 31, 1848:

> We have this day joined Canada with the United States by a cord, half an inch in diameter, and are making preparations to extend a foot bridge across by the 1st of June. Our shanties are erected, and we have a large number of men at work. Everything looks like going ahead. . . . Men are very busy in laying out the town of Bellevue, and are making arrangements for putting up a large hotel. The situation is a beautiful one, and bids fair in the opinion of many to surpass the town at the Falls.[4]

I don't think Charles Ellet Jr. ever imagined the impact his bridge would have. I'm not sure that Homan Walsh even cared. But their efforts enabled millions of honeymooners, like my mom and dad, to steal a kiss. And it all started with one kite string! It always does, doesn't it? As God said to the prophet Zechariah, "Do not despise these small beginnings, for the LORD rejoices to see the work begin, to see the plumb line in Zerubbabel's hand."[5] Plumb line, kite string—same difference!

Does God delight in our accomplishments? Like a proud parent. And not just the big accomplishments! According to this verse from Zechariah, it's the little things that produce disproportionate celebration. The Israelites hadn't even broken ground on the temple yet. All they'd done was measure, and God was already giving them a standing ovation! Our heavenly Father celebrates the little steps of faith, the small acts of kindness. In fact, you can't give someone a drink of water without God taking notice! God is great not just because nothing is *too big*. God is great because nothing is *too small*.

Now let me flip that script.

I know people who say they'll give more when they make more. I'm not buying what they're selling. I know people who say they'll serve more when they have more time. We've already debunked that myth. You don't *find* time; you *make* time! And I know people who think they'll be ready to step up when the *big* opportunity presents itself. Not if they aren't taking advantage of little opportunities right here, right now!

How you do *anything* is how you'll do *everything*.

We want to do amazing things for God, but that isn't our job. Our job is to consecrate ourselves to God. Then God does amazing things for us. It starts with the fourth habit—*fly the kite*. It's doing little things like they're big things. Go ahead and dream big, but start small. The good news? If you do little things like they're big things, God will do big things like they're little things. That's how kite strings turn into suspension bridges.

If you aren't making little sacrifices right now, you aren't ready.

If you aren't taking little risks right now, you aren't ready.

When National Community Church took its first mission trip in 2001, we couldn't even field an entire team, so we tag-teamed with another church. In the last decade, more than three thousand people have taken 273 mission trips. During that time, we've given more than $20 million to missions. How did it start? With a fifty-dollar check in 1996. My point? Don't despise the day of small beginnings.

Little by little, bad habits are broken.

Little by little, good habits are built.

Little by little, dreams become reality.

It's time to fly the kite!

7

Make Each Day a Masterpiece

Sweat the small stuff.

From 1964 to 1975, the UCLA Bruins dominated college basketball, winning ten NCAA national championships. They won seven of those championships in a *row*! Do you know how hard it is to win back-to-back championships? Back to back to back to back to back to back to back is unbelievable! Six times John Wooden was named College Basketball Coach of the Year. The Wizard of Westwood ranks as one of the most revered coaches in the history of sports, yet those who knew John Wooden would argue that his character off the court was even more impressive than his coaching on it.

John Wooden's college coaching career began at Indiana State Teachers College. After winning the Indiana Intercollegiate Conference title in 1947, his team received an invitation to compete in the NAIB National Tournament. Wooden rejected the invitation because of the NAIB policy banning black players. One of Wooden's players, Clarence Walker, was African American. If all his players could not compete, none of them would.

Wooden's team made it to the National Tournament final the next year, where they lost to Louisville. It was the only championship game ever lost by a Wooden-coached team, but he had already won a moral victory. John Wooden's refusal to play the year before was the catalyst that caused the NAIB to reverse their policy banning black players. Clarence Walker became the first African American to play in a post-season intercollegiate basketball tournament.[1]

Like those of most coaches I know, John Wooden's career was full of twists and turns. In fact, it took a twist of fate for him to end up at UCLA. His first choice was the University of Minnesota. After interviewing with both schools, Wooden arranged for a 6:00 p.m. call with Minnesota and a 7:00 p.m. call with UCLA on the same day. Wooden planned on accepting Minnesota's offer and declining the offer from UCLA. Unfortunately for the Golden Gophers, a snowstorm delayed the call from their athletic director, Frank McCormick. When he finally got through, it was too late. John Wooden had given his word to UCLA, and his word was his bond.[2]

Through all the ups and downs of life, the wins and the losses, it was a seven-point creed that served as John Wooden's compass. It was his rule of life. John Wooden's father introduced him to the creed, but it wasn't original to Joshua Wooden. He copied the creed from a 1931 interview with Supreme Court Justice John H. Clarke.[3] Wooden's version looked like this:

1. Be true to yourself.
2. Help others.
3. Make each day your masterpiece.
4. Drink deeply from good books, especially the Bible.
5. Make friendship a fine art.
6. Build a shelter against a rainy day.
7. Pray for guidance, and count and give thanks for your blessings every day.

I love all seven, but we'll focus on number three. What does it mean to *make each day a masterpiece*? The answer for each person, of course, is as different as each of us. You need to come up with your own answer, and you'll have different answers during different seasons of life.

If you want to win the day, you've got to define the win: *What's important now*? I'll help you identify lead measures and lag measures in the next chapter. But before you define the win, you've got to define success itself.

THE LADDER OF SUCCESS

Many people are so busy climbing the ladder of success that they fail to realize it's leaning against the wrong wall.[4] They fly their kites whichever direction the wind is blowing. Everybody wants to be successful, but few people know when they've actually achieved success. Why? If you don't define success, you never know whether you've hit the target.

Most of us default to a cultural definition, which often amounts to keeping up with the Kardashians. "We buy things we don't need," said Dave Ramsey, "with money we don't have in order to impress people we don't like."[5] Instead of living our lives, we try to live up to everybody else's expectations. That is quite the burden to bear. That kind of "success" is a recipe for failure. Get off that merry-go-round as fast as you can, no matter which horse you're riding!

Success is multidimensional, so it's okay to have multiple definitions. And those definitions may change during different seasons of life. In the grand scheme of things, success is stewardship, and stewardship is success. Simply put, *success is doing the best you can with what you have where you are*. Potential is God's gift to us, and what we do with it is our gift to God. That's the bottom line. Quit comparing yourself with everyone else. Are you becoming the best version of yourself possible? Are you making the most of the unique gifts God has given you? Are you working on your weak hand? Are you swimming laps?

When we define success, it's helpful to think in terms of different categories. Financially, success is raising your standard of giving rather than your standard of living. Spiritually, success is glorifying God and enjoying Him forever. Relationally, success is when those who know you best respect you most. At the end of the day, I want to be famous in my home. I love pastoring and writing, but success is not measured by church size or sales numbers.

If you succeed at the wrong thing, you've failed.

If you fail at the right thing, you've succeeded.

What is your definition of success? Spiritually? Relationally? Financially? Professionally? How will you know when you've achieved it? When it comes to defining success, it helps to detail your ideal day. And I don't mean your ideal vacation. I'm all for vacations, but you should love the life you go back to! In the regular routine of life, how does your ideal day start? What time is it? Where are you? Who are you with? And what are you doing? Does your ideal day, like mine, include a nap? A workout? Margin to read? Time to listen—really listen—to your spouse?

Here's the reality: most of us don't get what we want because we don't really know what we want. We spend more time planning a one-week vacation than the rest of our lives. Once you define your ideal day, you can identify the lead measures that will produce the results you want.

Before we go any further, let's go back to the beginning—the very beginning.

ORIGINAL INTENT

Each day of creation in Genesis was a masterpiece, was it not? Pick a day, any day—flowers blooming and trees bearing fruit on day three; the sun setting and moon rising on day four; fish swimming and birds flying on day five. At the end of each day, God stepped back and admired His handiwork. There is a common refrain: "God saw that it was good."[6]

God made each day a masterpiece—literally! Then the Creator stepped back on day six, and it's almost like He exceeded His own expectations, if that is even possible. "Behold, it was very good."[7]

I know it's easy to get frustrated by everything that isn't going according to plan. I know it's easy to get distracted by all the sideways energy.

Can I remind you of a few facts?

Planet Earth is spinning at one thousand miles per hour while speeding through space at sixty-six thousand miles per hour. How do we not get dizzy? Your ability to maintain balance is absolutely astounding! And even on days when you feel like you didn't get much done, you did travel 1.6 million miles through space!

We each take about twenty-three thousand breaths every day, which means we owe God twenty-three thousand thank-yous. By the way, some Hebrew scholars believe that the name of God, *Yahweh—YHWH* without the vowels—is the sound of breath. That's a beautiful thought, isn't it? On one hand, His name is too sacred to pronounce. On the other hand, it's whispered with every breath we take. It's our first word, our last word, and every word in between.

Your heart will beat more than one hundred thousand times today, circulating five quarts of blood through one hundred thousand miles of arteries and veins and capillaries.[8] Thirty-seven sextillion chemical reactions are happening in your body at any given time. And the combined DNA in all the cells in your body could stretch to the sun and back sixty-one times.[9]

There are no ordinary people!

There are no ordinary things!

There are no ordinary days!

When patrons walk into the Miracle Theatre on Capitol Hill, which we own and operate, they are greeted by something Albert Einstein said: "There are only two ways to live your life. One is as though nothing is a miracle. The other is as though everything is."[10] In case you haven't guessed, I subscribe to the second school of thought. If you want to win the day and make it into a masterpiece, you've got to start by recognizing it for what it is. Every day is nothing short of a miracle!

CELEBRATE THE BIG STUFF

God set a precedent with each day of creation. Each day was as different from the next as, well, night and day. Let me have a little fun and liken each day to one of my favorite memories. Day one is like standing on Main Street at Disney World and watching the Electrical Parade go by. Day two is the splash zone at SeaWorld. Day three is the Boerner Botanical Gardens in Milwaukee, Wisconsin. Day four is the Adler Planetarium in downtown Chicago. Day five is swimming with sea lions in the Galápagos Islands. Day six? This one is tough. God created humankind in His own image. The closest I can come is the moment each of our three children took their first breath.

Each creation day was its own one-of-a-kind, never-to-be-repeated masterpiece! Isn't that the way it's supposed to be? The first chapter of Genesis reveals God's original intent. Sure, we all have terrible, horrible, no good, very bad days.[11] Of course, God is hovering over the chaos now just like He was then. He's quite capable of making something beautiful out of even the bad days.

I know that sounds very theological, very philosophical. I promise you, we'll get painfully practical. But until you recognize each day for what it is—the first day and last day of your life—it's all for naught. The best way to steward every moment and make each day into a masterpiece is to recognize each day as miraculous.

Teddy Roosevelt had a nighttime ritual that is worth emulating. It was like an exclamation mark at the end of his ideal day. He and his naturalist friend, William Beebe, had a habit of going outside and looking into the star-filled sky. After using the Great Square of Pegasus to locate the Andromeda Galaxy, Roosevelt would recite the following: "That is the Spiral Galaxy in Andromeda. It is as large as our Milky Way. It is one of a hundred million galaxies. It is 750,000 light-years away. It consists of one hundred billion suns, each larger than our sun." He would pause, then grin and say, "Now I think we are small enough! Let's go to bed."[12]

The creation story is a microcosm of so many things. God said, "Let there be light,"[13] and those words are still creating galaxies at the edge of the universe. If God can do that with just those words, what are we worried about? We already trust Him for the big things like keeping the planets in orbit. All we need to do now is trust Him for the little things, which is everything else by comparison!

Speaking of little things, how many species of ants do you think there are? If you've seen one ant, you've seen them all. Right? Not quite! Entomologists have identified at least twelve thousand species! That borders on creative overkill, doesn't it? My favorite species is the Sahara desert ant, which is able to move at a speed of 2.8 feet per second—108 times its body length. I did the math, and that's ten times faster than the fastest human. Of course, the number of ant species don't even begin to compare with 350,000 species of beetles! Suffice it to say, *God loves variety*! Again, God is great not just because nothing is *too big*. God is great because nothing is *too small*.

That's what flying the kite is all about—doing little things like they're big things! While we're on the subject, that's what ants are all about. Solomon said, "Go to the ant, you sluggard; consider its ways and be wise!"[14] When we do little things like they're big things, we're taking a page out of *A Bug's Life*.

Go ahead and dream big, but start small.

SWEAT THE SMALL STUFF

As John Wooden approached his one hundredth birthday, he shared a well-worn observation: "'Make *each* day your masterpiece.' When you do that as the weeks and months and years . . . unfold behind you, you'll have the deepest self-satisfaction knowing your life has really meant something. You will have achieved the most important kind of success, namely, becoming the best that you are capable of becoming."[15]

How do you become the greatest coach of all time?[16] How do you start and sustain an eighty-eight-game winning streak? How do you win 620 games with only 147 losses?

It starts with you putting on your socks, one foot at a time. At least, that's how former all-American Bill Walton remembered his first day of practice. The first thing Coach Wooden did was call his new recruits into the locker room. Walton was waiting for the Wizard of Westwood to cast a spell and hand them the keys to the basketball kingdom. His first words? "Men, this is how you put your shoes and socks on."

"We were stunned," said Walton. "Are you kidding me? We're all high school All-American players, and here is this silly little old man showing us how to put on our shoes and socks!" And Wooden didn't stop there. After demonstrating the way they were to pull up their socks—no folds, no wrinkles, no creases of any kind—he taught them how to properly lace their shoes. He also showed them how to tuck in their jerseys and knot the drawstrings of their shorts.[17] Coach Wooden made no assumptions!

The question, of course, is, Why? Like every great coach, I think John Wooden knew that how you do *anything* is how you'll do *everything*. How you practice is how you'll play in the game! Coach Wooden explained, "These seemingly trivial matters, taken together and added to many, many other so-called trivial matters build into something very big: namely, your success."[18]

There is a proverb, centuries old. Its origin is difficult to determine, but I wonder whether it inspired Wooden's sock hop.

> For want of a nail, the shoe was lost.
> For want of a shoe, the horse was lost.
> For want of a horse, the rider was lost.
> For want of a rider, the message was lost.
> For want of a message, the battle was lost.
> For want of a battle, the kingdom was lost.
> And all for the want of a horseshoe nail.

The devil is not in the details; God is! Did you know that nine chapters in the book of Exodus are devoted to the aesthetics of the tabernacle? They detail the color of the curtains, the formula for incense, and the arrangement of the furniture. In God's economy, little things are big things! Jesus said it this way: "If you are faithful in little things, you will be faithful in large ones."[19]

Two Hundred Pomegranates

In the fourth year of his reign as king of Israel, Solomon commenced construction of the temple in Jerusalem. Despite employing 150,000 skilled laborers, it took seven years to knock out the punch list. The project required tons of timber, so King Solomon negotiated a trade deal with King Hiram of Tyre. King Hiram cut down trees and floated them like rafts down the coast of the Mediterranean Sea to a port city called Joppa. Then the logs were transported to Jerusalem and used to build Solomon's temple. Along with the logs, King Hiram sent an expert artisan named Huram. Let's call him Huram the Creator.

Extremely skilled in bronze craftsmanship, Huram cast two twenty-seven-foot pillars that would adorn the entrance to King Solomon's temple. He even named them—Boaz and Jakin. The columns were first-impression pieces. No one got inside without walking through them. Huram designed seven-and-a-half-foot capitals to place on top of the columns. And on top of the capitals, "200 pomegranates in two rows around them."[20]

So, Huram designed two hundred pomegranates for the capitals. So what? Who cares what the tops of the columns looked like? They were thirty-four and a half feet in the air. *No one was going to see them!* That, my friend, is the point. Only two people were going to notice this creative nuance. The first was the artist himself, Huram the Creator. The second was *the* Artist, *the* Creator.

I can't help but wonder whether those two hundred pomegranates were God's favorite feature. I can't prove it, but I bet Joseph pointed them out to Jesus when they visited the temple in His youth. Why? Because he was a craftsman and that's what craftsmen notice! *Son, look at the tops of those columns. Can You see them? Huram designed two hun-*

dred pomegranates on top of those columns, to the glory of God. Go Thou and do likewise. Maybe I'm getting a little carried away with the last sentence, but I love what Dorothy Sayers once said: "No crooked table legs or ill-fitting drawers ever, I dare swear, came out of the carpenter's shop at Nazareth."[21]

AUDIENCE OF ONE

If you are extrinsically motivated, you don't care about the things that no one else can see. It's all for show. What you care about is the press conference. You don't do anything without issuing a press release. I feel sorry for that kind of person because fame and fortune are awfully fickle.

If you are intrinsically motivated, all you care about is the audience of One. You do what you do for the applause of nail-scarred hands. You don't compare yourself with other people! Why? Because they aren't you and you aren't them. I have a hunch that Huram was functioning out of intrinsic motivation, not because Solomon was looking over his shoulder.

Have you heard the story of the three bricklayers? When asked what they were doing, the first bricklayer said, "I'm laying bricks." The second said, "I'm building a wall." The third said, "I'm constructing a cathedral to the glory of God." All three bricklayers were doing the same thing, but they were doing it for different reasons.

"Whatever you do, work at it with all your heart," said the apostle Paul, "as working for the Lord, not for human masters."[22] There it is again: how you do *anything* is how you'll do *everything*. Dr. Martin Luther King Jr. said it this way:

If it falls your lot to sweep streets in life, sweep streets like Michelangelo painted pictures. Sweep streets like Beethoven composed music. Sweep streets like Shakespeare wrote poetry. Sweep streets so well that all the hosts of heaven and earth will have to pause and say, "Here lived a great street sweeper, who swept his job well."[23]

Before the release of the feature film *A Beautiful Day in the Neighborhood,* I saw a behind-the-scenes interview with Joanne Rogers, Fred Rogers's wife of fifty years. Mr. Rogers modeled kindness and compassion to many generations of children, including mine. Over thirty-one seasons, he filmed 895 episodes and wrote more than 289 songs.[24] His way with children was unprecedented, unparalleled. How did Mr. Rogers have such a profound impact on so many? According to Joanne, Fred believed to the depth of his soul that the space between the television and the children watching it was holy ground. That explains a lot, doesn't it? That was his It factor, his X factor.

What is your holy ground?

I take off my shoes when I write because I consider writing to be holy ground—a sacred trinity of writer and reader and God. You are giving me five hours of your time, give or take. With God's help, I'm going to give you the best book I've got. Taking off my shoes is a ritual reminder that writing is a divine calling. I don't just type on a keyboard. I worship God with the twenty-six letters of the English alphabet.

Your employer may not appreciate you taking your shoes off at work, and that isn't necessary. Simply fly the kite with all your heart when no one is looking. The true measure of success is not doing a great job when you get your dream job. It's doing a great job at a job you don't like, for a boss you like even less!

LOVE OF THE GAME

In his last decade of life, John Wooden was asked what he missed most about coaching. His one-word answer? "Practice."[25] I find that fascinating but not surprising. Those who attain the highest levels of success are not motivated by accolades. Sure, they want to win the game, whatever game they play. But their ultimate goal is becoming better than they were the day before! How? Practice makes perfect—deliberate practice, that is.

No one loved the game of basketball more than Michael Jordan. In fact, he had a love-of-the-game clause added to his contract, allowing him to play pickup basketball whenever and wherever he wanted. Why is he the greatest player in NBA history? He loved the game more than anyone else! A close second to Michael Jordan is the late great Kobe Bryant.

A few years before his untimely death, I got a glimpse of Kobe Bryant's practice routine via performance coach Alan Stein. Alan spent fifteen years working with some of the highest-performing athletes on the planet. One day, Alan bumped into Kobe Bryant at a basketball camp and asked whether he could watch him work out. You have not because you ask not! Kobe told Alan to meet him at the gym at four o'clock. No, not in the afternoon. Alan showed up early, wanting to impress Kobe. Kobe was already in a full sweat, and he was doing the same drills he taught his campers. Alan questioned Kobe about what he believed to be a very basic, very boring workout. Kobe said, "Why do you think I'm the best in the world? I don't get bored with the basics."[26]

That explains everything, doesn't it?

Kobe Bryant applied his insane work ethic to everything he did. It's how he taught himself to play Beethoven's *Moonlight Sonata* by ear.[27] It's how he won an Academy Award for Best Animated Short Film. It's how he coached his daughter Gianna's basketball team.

Kobe did everything with the Mamba mentality: "It's a constant quest to try to [be] better today than you were yesterday."[28]

Kobe's award-winning film, *Dear Basketball*, was inspired by a love poem he wrote at the end of his career. It would have made John Wooden proud. Referring to his six-year-old self, Kobe said of basketball, "I fell in love with you."[29]

If you're going to make each day a masterpiece, you need to ultimately *love what you do* and *do what you love.* If your job isn't exactly your dream job, that can be frustrating. Can I offer a couple of suggestions to inch you closer to where you want to be? First of all, the jobs we don't like help us appreciate the ones we do! Few people land their dream jobs right away. Finding your sweet spot—the place where your God-given gifts and God-ordained passions overlap—involves trial and error. Second, the key to landing your dream job is doing a really *good job* at a really *bad job*. Remember Horst Schulze? Cleaning ashtrays isn't anybody's dream job. That's when you fly the kite! How? Focus on being faithful in the little things. If you keep putting on your socks the right way, your day will come.

"To think of me as a person that's overachieved," said Kobe, "that would mean a lot to me." Why? "That means I put a lot of work in and squeezed every ounce of juice out of this orange that I could."[30] Squeezing the orange. Flying the kite. Same difference! It's giving it everything you've got. And it's doing so until the day you die! Why? There is no finish line!

If you win the day that way, you will have won the game of life long before God says, "Well done, good and faithful servant!"[31] That's how you become the best version of yourself possible, and that's the definition of success.

8

Kaizen

If you do little things like they're big things,
God will do big things like they're little things.

Sakichi Toyoda was born on February 14, 1867, in a remote farming community in rural Japan. The son of a carpenter, Sakichi grew up in a sawdust-covered workshop. Like his father, he loved tinkering with anything. His passion for innovation would eventually earn him the moniker King of Japanese Inventors.

As a young man, Sakichi got his hands on *Self-Help*, a book first published in England in 1859.[1] Profiling some of history's greatest inventors, author Samuel Smiles championed the merits of self-help. How? By paying attention to absolutely everything.

One day, while watching the way his mother and grandmother labored on their manual looms, Sakichi was inspired to design a power-driven loom. Thus began Toyoda Automatic Loom Works. The driving force behind Sakichi's innovation was a trial-and-error tactic he called *genchi genbutsu*—"go and see."[2] A hands-on approach to problem-solving, it was the heart and soul of what would become known as the Toyota Way.

After World War II, the Japanese economy was devastated and the automobile company started by Sakichi's son was on the brink of bankruptcy. Its debt was eight times its capital value! Fast-forward seventy-five years, and Toyota's net worth is $236 billion.[3] What happened? The short answer is *kaizen,* an uncompromising commitment to continuous improvement. But the catalyst was a "go and see" field trip.

In 1950, Sakichi's nephew Eiji Toyoda took a team of engineers on a twelve-week tour of automobile plants in America. The Toyota team expected to be amazed. Instead, they were surprised by the inefficiencies they found in American assembly lines. With a bit of brazen—and a lot of kaizen—they believed they could beat America at the automobile game. Considering Toyota is now the largest automobile manufacturer in the world, it could be argued that they did just that.

No matter what you do, kaizen is key. It starts with a growth mindset. You've got to stay humble, stay hungry. You benchmark your progress, but you never really arrive. In fact, there is no finish line. You keep flying the kite a little higher, a little longer.

LITTLE BY LITTLE

There is a three-word phrase buried in the book of Exodus that produces mixed emotions for me: "Little by little."[4] Let me set the scene, then I'll explain the mixed emotions. The Israelites are getting ready to possess the Promised Land, but God throws a little monkey wrench in the plan. "I will not drive them out in a single year."[5] This is where mixed emotions enter the equation.

I like nonstop flights—economy plus, if possible! Are you picking up what I'm throwing down? I want to get where I want to go without any connections. Of course, it rarely works that way. This fact is evidenced by the Israelites' wilderness wanderings. The journey from Mount Sinai to the Promised Land was supposed to take eleven days, but it turned into a forty-year flight with forty-two stops.

I've had a few flights that have turned into—shall we say—adventures! After one of those travel debacles, which ended with me renting a car and driving through the night to get where I needed to go, I had a little revelation. No matter how many detours and delays we experience as modern-day travelers, *it still beats a covered wagon*! Am I right? That's the way I flip the script on frustrating flights!

The stations of the Exodus numbered forty-two! When the Israelites finally entered the Promised Land, I bet they wanted it to be a one-stop shop! Not so fast.

> Little by little I will drive them out before you, until you have increased enough to take possession of the land.[6]

God delivers us little by little.
God promotes us little by little.
God grows us little by little.

The question, of course, is, Why? In this instance, the reason was more ecological than theological. "Because the land would become desolate and the wild animals too numerous for you."[7] Let's be honest—our ability to anticipate consequences is unreliable at best. God has reasons that are beyond human reason. That's hard for us to accept, but we resist at our own risk.

We hate playing the waiting game, especially if it's the dating game. We want God to deliver on His promises *yesterday*! We plant on Monday and want to harvest on Tuesday. News flash to nonfarmers: it takes a little longer than that. "Don't judge each day by the harvest you reap," said Robert Louis Stevenson, "but by the seeds that you plant."

DESIRABLE DIFFICULTY

Before we go any further, let me give you a formula. Formulas tend to become formulaic, but it's a risk I'm willing to take. Please understand that your unique history, personality, and goals are the X factor in this equation.

Deliberate Practice + Desirable Difficulty = Durable Learning[8]

We drilled down on the idea of deliberate practice when we explored ambidexterity. It's time to unpack desirable difficulty. Sounds like an oxymoron, doesn't it? What's desirable about difficulty? At first glance, nothing! Upon further review, everything.

"Look at a day when you are supremely satisfied at the end," said Margaret Thatcher. "It's not a day when you lounge around doing nothing; it's a day you've had everything to do and you've done it."[9] We hate to admit it, but the former British prime minister is as spot on as a spot of tea. Sure, we need some zero-gravity days. It's called the Sabbath. But rest is best after hard work!

Coined by Robert A. Bjork in 1994, *desirable difficulty* refers to a task that requires considerable effort.[10] Difficult tasks slow down the learning process at first but yield greater long-term benefits than easy tasks.[11] If something is too easy, we get bored. If something is too difficult, we quit. There is a middle ground where growth happens. As I've already noted, it's called JMD—*just manageable difficulty.*

As I see it, my job as a pastor is to *comfort the afflicted* and *afflict the comfortable.* The former is far easier than the latter but not nearly as important. Comforting the afflicted results in warm fuzzies, but that isn't how spiritual battles are won or lost. Afflicting the comfortable may not get me gift cards during pastor appreciation month, but that is how spiritual growth happens. Tell me the last time you were uncomfortable, and I'll tell you the last time you grew! The idea of desirable difficulty is nothing new.

> Consider it pure joy, my brothers and sisters, whenever you face trials of many kinds, because you know that the testing of your faith produces perseverance. Let perseverance finish its work so that you may be mature and complete, not lacking anything.[12]

As a parent, my natural bent is to make it easier on my kids. But you and I both know that's not doing our kids any favors! If everyone gets a trophy, how will kids learn how to manage failure? If we bail them out of every difficulty, their emotional muscles will atrophy.

When we go through tough times, God is building emotional fortitude in us. He is preparing us for bigger and better things. The challenges that seem incredibly difficult now will seem like a cakewalk in ten years!

If you "help" a butterfly escape its chrysalis, you actually hurt it. It will never fly the kite. You've got to let your kids go through chrysalis, just like God does with us. It's called tough love. It's letting them learn how to stand on their own feet. Go ahead and toddler-proof your outlets, but you've got to let them take a few tumbles!

STRETCH GOALS

I live by a little mantra: "Harder is better." I know—harder is harder too! I don't want to give the impression that I never choose the path of least resistance. I usually take the escalator instead of the stairs. That said, taking the stairs is a great way to habit stack if you're getting ready to hike the Grand Canyon.

One of my top-of-the-Empire-State-Building moments was standing on the south rim of the Grand Canyon and looking over the canyon I had just crossed with my older son, Parker. It was his rite-of-passage hike, and it's one of the hardest things I've ever done. The harder the hike, the better the view! The most gratifying goals always involve the highest degree of difficulty!

A few years ago, I was inspired by a sentence from the Psalms: "They go from strength to strength, till each appears before God in Zion."[13] With the help of a friend who happens to be a strength and conditioning coach, I experimented with this idea in a rather unique way. At the time, twenty-five proper-form push-ups was my out-of-shape ceiling. I decided to add one push-up every day, with the goal of hitting one hundred. Sure, I missed a day here and there. Flying the kite is not a perfect science! But seventy-five days later, I hit my goal of one hundred consecutive push-ups.

By definition, stretch goals are "little by little." That's how you go "from strength to strength." Over time, your ceiling becomes your floor. What seemed impossible ten years ago now feels like a walk in the park! It's as simple as setting stretch goals, which brings me all the way back to my marathon. If you start too fast, you'll finish slow! You've got to pace yourself, which is the genius of kaizen. It's adding one rep, one pound, one lap per day.

I could barely run three miles when I started training for the Chicago Marathon, and I ran *really* slow. I could hardly imagine running 26.2 miles. What did I do? I downloaded a training plan; then I worked the plan. Over a six-month span, I completed seventy-two training runs totaling 475 miles. Then—and only then—was I ready to run my marathon.

GODSPEED

Remember Emil Zátopek? The greatest runner of all time? While turning his life story into a movie script, I analyzed his running rituals. Emil Zátopek was ordinary in every way. He measured five foot seven on tiptoes and weighed 145 pounds soaking wet. He possessed little natural talent, and his running style was hopelessly unorthodox. Sportswriters said he ran like a man who had been stabbed in the heart, a man who had scorpions in his shoes, a man who was wrestling an octopus on a conveyor belt. That didn't keep the Czech Locomotive from doing what will never be done again.

Emil Zátopek won triple gold in the 1952 Helsinki Olympics, setting Olympic records in the five thousand meter, ten thousand meter, and marathon. From 1949 to 1951, he won sixty-nine consecutive races. That may be more impressive than UCLA's eighty-eight-game winning streak. And he would end his career with eighteen world records.

How did Emil do what he did? His 1951 military file highlighted one defining characteristic—"doggedness."[14] Many runners were faster than Emil, but no one trained longer or harder or smarter. He never stopped setting stretch goals, always trying to beat his personal best. He took pride in his accomplishments, but he also made an admission: "Whoever surpasses my training will also break my records."[15]

While on sentry duty, Emil would run in place in combat boots for hours. During training runs, he would wear a gas mask to deprive himself of oxygen. He often carried his wife, Dana, on his back or pulled her through the snow on a sled. He may not have invented interval training, but he reinvented it. And Emil ran so hard for so long that he passed out on the track more than once.

After eighteen years of competitive running, Emil hung his running shoes from a nail in the wall of his living room. He had run more than fifty thousand miles—the equivalent of two laps around the world. Emil Zátopek embodied kaizen. "You cannot jump to the second floor from the pavement," he said. "Step by step, though, a man will come to the fifth floor."[16]

At this point, you might be wondering why so few people have heard of Emil Zátopek. In November 1969, he was sent to the uranium mines for courageously resisting Soviet occupation. "I have already got to know the world from on high," he said. "Now I am getting to know it from down below."[17] Emil would spend the next five years doing forced labor.

The Communist regime did all they could to erase Emil Zátopek's name from history. His name was removed from the stadium in his hometown of Kopřivnice. His athletic accomplishments were deleted from textbooks. They tried to bury him 150 meters below ground in a uranium mine, but Emil Zátopek's legacy outlasted the Soviet Union itself. His athletic achievements merit the silver screen. Even more, his uncompromising character deserves to be celebrated.

We love success stories like Emil Zátopek's. The sacrifices that made them possible—not so much. We want success without sacrifice, but it doesn't work that way. At the heart of every success story is someone who was willing to make sacrifices that no one else was willing to. Success will not be shortchanged, and it never goes on sale.

One of the hardest pills to swallow in the Gospels is this one: "Whoever wants to be my disciple must deny themselves and take up their cross daily and follow me."[18] The best decision you can make *for* yourself is making decisions *against* yourself. It's disciplining yourself to do the right things day in and day out, week in and week out, year in and year out. If you pay the price, the payoff will be far greater than the sacrifices you made.

LEAD MEASURES

One key to kaizen—uncompromising commitment to continuous improvement—is feedback loops. The most effective feedback loop is the conviction of the Holy Spirit. Scripture serves the same function. We don't read it as much as it reads us! Of course, feedback loops are only as effective as self-evaluation.

A good place to start is with a SWOT analysis. SWOT stands for "strengths, weaknesses, opportunities, and threats." This kind of analysis is often employed in organizations, but it's a healthy exercise when it comes to self-evaluation. After listing your strengths, weaknesses, opportunities, and threats, you've got to define the win: *What's important now?*

Lag measures are outcomes. They're quarterly earnings and customer satisfaction. They're wins. Grades. Poll numbers. Lag measures are targets—the bull's-eyes you're aiming at. You want to win the game, win the sale, win the election. But lag measures are not how you get where you want to go. That's where lead measures come into play. Lead measures are the best practices that will produce the results you want.

If you want to lose weight, you have to make decisions against yourself. I'd recommend locking in a specific goal. If you don't define your target weight, you won't know when you've reached it. You're setting yourself up to lose, and I don't mean weight. You also need a plan, and there are plenty of them out there. Diet plans are above my pay grade, so I won't overstep my bounds. My only expertise is the Grand Canyon diet. If you hike the Grand Canyon in 110-degree heat, you can lose thirteen pounds in two days!

Just to put your mind at ease, I know that not everybody is a goal setter. And that's okay. Some people are problem solvers. Can I let you in on a little secret? Goal setting and problem-solving are two sides of the same coin.

Winning the day is as unique as the job you have, the person you're married to, and the goals you set. It's as unique as the medical challenges you face, the God-ordained passions you're pursuing, and the crazy circumstances you find yourself in. You cannot win the day for anyone else, and no one else can win the day for you.

One warning: don't try to win the whole world. Remember, your goals have got to be defined by JMD—*just manageable difficulty*. You've got to take it one goal, one game, one project, one workout, one mile, one day at a time.

During the 2019 Major League Baseball season, the Washington Nationals found themselves in last place in the National League East. With a record of 19–31, their odds of making the postseason were 3.8 percent. The odds of winning the NL pennant? Only .1 percent. That's when their manager, Dave Martinez, challenged the team with a simple idea that would become their team theme: "go 1–0 today." At that point, the Nats had nothing to lose! Why not go out and have some fun? That mindset took them all the way to a World Series championship![19]

If you want to fly the pennant, you need to fly the kite. How? By committing yourself to kaizen. By embracing desirable difficulty as a gift from God. By setting stretch goals. By making decisions against yourself. By defining the win.

Fly the kite!

PART THREE

Imagine Unborn Tomorrows

Everything that exists was once an idea in someone's imagination. Before becoming a physical reality, it was an electrochemical signal firing across billions of synapses within the cerebral cortex.

The layout of the city where I live—Washington, DC—first existed in the mind of a French-born architect named Pierre-Charles L'Enfant. The military engineer turned urban planner was commissioned by George Washington to lay out the nation's capital. The symmetry of the streets and the location of government buildings were conceived in his imagination. After imagining every detail, L'Enfant transferred those ideas to a twenty-ounce piece of paper, which now sits enshrined in a Plexiglas case, breathing pressurized argon at the Library of Congress.

When I negotiate traffic on Pennsylvania Avenue, I am driving down streets that L'Enfant dreamed up. The same is true when we picnic on the National Mall or I run by the Lincoln Memorial. My physical reality was someone else's idea. That's true for you too. In fact, it's true *of* you.

Everything that exists originated in the omniscient imagination of the Almighty. It was a thought before it became a thing, and that includes you. You were once an idea in the imagination of God. Hold that thought—pun intended.

Take captive every thought to make it obedient to Christ.[1]

We tend to interpret that verse in negative terms. Take sinful thoughts captive and make them obedient to Christ. That is half the battle, but let me flip that script. I'd rather have one God idea than a thousand good ideas. Good ideas are good, but God ideas change the course of history. How do you get God ideas? Prayer is a good place to start. Praying is a form of dreaming, and dreaming is a form of praying.

When you get a God idea, you've got to take it captive. How? That depends on what you do. If you're Pierre-Charles L'Enfant, it's a blueprint. If you're David Blaine, it's a magic trick. If you're Twyla Tharp, it's a choreography. If you're Mozart, it's a musical score. If you're John Wooden, it's a game plan. You get the idea.

When I sit down to write, I am imagining unborn tomorrows. The way I take those thoughts captive is with the twenty-six letters of the English alphabet. I don't know what you do, but whatever it is, you have to imagine unborn tomorrows. If you're a chef, it's planning a menu. You have to take those ingredients captive and plate them. If you're an entrepreneur, it's developing a business plan. You have to take that product captive and brand it and sell it.

In part 3, we turn our full attention to the future. It's time to explore the habits that will help you imagine unborn tomorrows—*cut the rope* and *wind the clock*. We live our lives forward, but God is working in our lives backward. "We are God's workmanship, created in Christ Jesus to do good works, which God prepared in advance."[2] Translation? God is setting you up. When God gives a vision, He makes provision!

According to the Talmud, along with everything God spoke into existence during the six days of creation, God made certain provisions. He commanded the Red Sea to split apart for Israel; the sun and moon to stand still for Joshua; the ravens to feed Elijah; the fish to spit out Jonah; the fire not to burn Hananiah, Mishael, and Azariah; and the lions not to harm Daniel.[3]

Four dimensions of space-time is all we've ever known, so it's very hard for us to conceive of God in any other way. What do we do? We create God in our image and make Him four-dimensional. News flash: God does not exist within the space-time dimensions He created. So while we think forward, God is working backward. It's a bit of a mind bender, but God always begins with the end in mind. That's key when it comes to imagining unborn tomorrows.

Remember L'Enfant? It's one thing to have an idea. It's another thing to turn it into reality. It has taken hundreds of years for his ideas to take shape. It has also taken tons of concrete and millions of dollars! No matter what you do, it'll take blood, sweat, and tears. The good news? God is "able to do immeasurably more than all we ask or imagine."[4]

God's vision for your life is bigger and better than yours! Do you believe that? Show me the size of your dream, and I'll show you the size of your God.

Habit 5—Cut the Rope

Playing it safe is risky.

In 1853, America hosted its first world's fair in New York City. The organizers built a beautiful exhibition hall called the Crystal Palace. This is where the latest and greatest inventions were showcased. This is also where a man named Elisha Otis pulled off one of the most remarkable stunts in the history of the world's fair. Otis was the inventor of the safety elevator brake, but he was having a hard time selling his idea to safety-first skeptics. It was time to go big or go home. He stood on an elevator platform hoisted high enough for everybody in the exhibition hall to see him. Then Otis, who had positioned an axman above the elevator, cued him to cut the rope!

The elevator fell—a few feet. The crowd let out a collective gasp. And Elisha Otis pronounced, "All safe, ladies and gentlemen. All safe."

I know—cutting the rope doesn't seem safe. Can I tell you what's not safe? Playing it safe! In fact, the greatest risk is taking no risks. Cutting the rope is about taking calculated risks. When I say "calculated," I'm talking about a risk-reward ratio. I'm not advocating blind leaps. Keep both eyes wide open, but you'd better not focus on the wind and waves. The only way to walk on water is to keep your eyes fixed on Jesus! Well, you have to get out of the boat too![1]

When Elisha Otis pulled off this unforgettable sales pitch, there were only a few buildings in New York City taller than five floors. Why? No one wanted to climb the stairs! It was next to impossible to rent top-floor real estate. Then in 1854, Otis installed an elevator in a building on Broadway, and the rest is history.

By 1890, there were ten buildings taller than ten stories. By 1900, there were sixty-five buildings taller than twenty stories. And by 1908, there were 538 buildings in New York City that qualified as skyscrapers, including the famous Flatiron Building between Broadway and Fifth Avenue. More and more buildings got taller and taller, and something else happened. Higher floors started producing higher revenues! As long as you didn't have to climb the stairs, everyone wanted a room with a view.

Elisha Otis had turned the world upside down. He didn't just invent the safety elevator brake; he made the modern skyscraper possible!

At last count, New York City has fifty-eight thousand elevators. Those elevators make eleven billion trips every year.[2] And that's just New York City! According to the Otis Elevator Company, the equivalent of the world's population rides on their products every three days.[3] All because Elisha Otis had the courage to cut the rope!

If you want to imagine unborn tomorrows, you've got to *cut the rope.* It's scary, especially if you're afraid of heights. But anything less is maintaining the status quo. You will experience a few falls, a few fails. That's for certain. But cutting the rope is the way we cut the ribbon on the dreams God has given us.

9

The Adjacent Possible

You are one decision away from a totally different life.

S tanding 1,046 feet tall, the Chrysler Building held the distinction of being the world's tallest building before being unseated by the Empire State Building. It still stands as one of New York City's most iconic skyscrapers. The building was the brainchild of Walter Chrysler, founder of the automobile empire bearing his name. His original goal was to top the Eiffel Tower, but he wasn't alone in his aspiration.

The architects of the Chrysler Building and the Bank of Manhattan Trust Building—partners turned rivals William van Alen and H. Craig Severance—engaged in a game of one-upmanship. They vied to earn their buildings the title of tallest in the world. Van Alen had an ace up his sleeve, a 125-foot spire that was constructed in secrecy and assembled in midair by the derring-do of high-wire construction workers.

During the Roaring Twenties, real estate values went through the roof. The Race to the Sky, as it was dubbed by newspapers, was fueled by unbridled optimism. Well, optimism and ego. "It was about hubris," said Neal Bascomb. "It was about making the world know what a success they were."[1] Walter Chrysler admitted as much to his architect: "I want to build a monument to me."[2] Chrysler got his monument, but the thrill of victory lasted all of one day!

The Chrysler Building was crowned the tallest building in the world on October 23, 1929. Do you by chance remember what happened the next day? October 24 marked the beginning of the Great Crash, which bankrupted many building owners and led to the Great Depression.

As we get ready to imagine unborn tomorrows, I begin with a cautionary tale. Why? We overestimate our ability to predict the future, and we do so often. This tendency goes by a lot of names—the law of unintended consequences, the overconfidence effect, and the planning fallacy, just to name a few.

Besides serving as a cautionary tale, this piece of history brings to mind an old proverb: "Do not boast about tomorrow, for you do not know what a day may bring."[3] Go ahead and make plans. Failing to plan is planning to fail, but planning without praying is called presumption!

Imagining unborn tomorrows begins and ends with prayer. I might add, brave prayer.

GROUND FLOOR

All that stands between you and your best unborn tomorrows is *the adjacent possible*. The phrase was coined by an evolutionary biologist named Stuart Kauffman,[4] and it's the elevator between *what is* and *what could be*. It's the thing that enables us to prayerfully dream bigger dreams—10-story dreams, 20-story dreams, even 160-story dreams like the Burj Khalifa.

I'm not sure Elisha Otis could have imagined a building half a mile tall, but he made it possible the day he cut the rope. Did you know that the Burj Khalifa is so tall that you can watch the sunset twice? You can watch the sunset from ground level, then catch a ride on one of sixty-five Otis elevators that will take you to the top floor at a speed of twenty-two miles per hour, and you can watch the sunset a second time. It gives you a second chance at the sun not setting on your anger![5]

The adjacent possible is not an easy concept to articulate, but the elevator is exhibit A. It was the elevator that made the skyscraper possible! As such, it opened up the adjacent possible. The elevator is to the skyscraper what the alphabet is to writing. The elevator is to the skyscraper what the acorn is to the oak tree. The elevator is to the skyscraper what Chicago deep dish is to pizza, but I digress.

Let me go back down to the ground floor.

The adjacent possible is the thing that makes something else possible. The microchip is the thing that made scientific calculators, personal computers, and smartphones possible. Without it, many of us wouldn't have passed math class! And we definitely wouldn't have landed a man on the moon. The adjacent possible is one small step that turns into a giant leap.

PLAN B

Let me personalize the adjacent possible.

When I was in the eighth grade, our family started attending Calvary Church in Naperville, Illinois. I had no idea that the pastor of that church, Bob Schmidgall, had a daughter. I didn't care in junior high, but that changed in high school when I cut the rope and asked her out on our first date. I had no idea at the time, but when our family started attending Calvary Church, Lora became the adjacent possible! So did our three children—Parker, Summer, and Josiah. So did a thousand other things!

While I was in graduate school, Lora and I tried to plant a church in the northern suburbs of Chicago. That church plant failed, and it was awfully embarrassing. We think of failure in negative terms, but failure isn't all bad. It's often the thing that introduces us to the adjacent possible by opening us up to options we would have never considered otherwise. If that church plant in Chicago had not failed, we would have never made the move to Washington, DC.

On that note, we'll someday thank God for the doors He *closed* as much as the ones He *opened*. Why? They introduce us to the adjacent possible. Closed doors are God's way of cutting the rope for us! If God had not closed the door to Bithynia, the apostle Paul may have never taken the gospel to Macedonia.[6] At the time, Macedonia seemed like a detour to him. Bithynia was plan A.

Sometimes our plan B is God's plan A.

Remember Pixar and their failed business model? Animation software was their plan A. When that failed, the adjacent possible was *Toy Story, Finding Nemo,* and my personal favorite, *Up.* Pretty good plan B—as in billions of dollars!

If you can't make ends meet or your latest venture ended in failure, maybe God is getting you ready for what He wants you to do next. When we feel like we're in the wrong place at the wrong time, God often has us right where He wants us!

For Lora and me, Chicago was plan A. We had a twenty-five-year plan for that church plant. If you want to make God laugh, tell Him your plans! God closed the door on our dream, and I'm eternally grateful. We had no intention of ever leaving Chicago. Michael Jordan was still playing for the Chicago Bulls. Why would we have wanted to leave?

Oftentimes God is setting us up, even when it feels like He is letting us down. It was our move to the nation's capital that made National Community Church the adjacent possible.

GAME ON

Everything I believe, as a follower of Christ, hinges on an empty tomb. When Jesus walked out of the tomb, impossible went out the window. This is where we begin imagining unborn tomorrows.

The cross is where God put His love on full display.

The empty tomb is where God put His power on full display.

Christianity is *not* a moral code. Yes, there is a Great Commandment. Love God with all your heart and soul and mind and strength, and love your neighbor as yourself.[7] Yes, we live by a code called the Sermon on the Mount—go the extra mile, turn the other cheek, love your enemies, and pray for those who persecute you.[8] That rule of life will change your life, but it's not the foundation of our faith. The foundation of our faith is an empty tomb.

I can't prove the Resurrection any more than you can disprove it. It's a tenet of faith, one way or the other. But if Jesus walked out of the tomb, all bets are off. And if you are in Christ, it means you can do all things through Him.[9]

Can I tell you why I'm so certain that you can win the day? Because Jesus won the day two thousand years ago! Just when it seemed like it was *game over,* it was *game on.* Never put a period where God puts a comma! Why? Jesus *is* the Adjacent Possible!

When Jesus arrived on the scene, no one had a category for the miracles He would perform. His first miracle happened at a wedding reception in Cana. The bridal party ran out of wine, which wasn't the end of the world. That said, it was awfully embarrassing for the bride and groom. What did Jesus do? He cut the rope, turning water into wine. And not just wine—fine wine![10] That's impossible! Right? Wrong! Why? Because Jesus is the Adjacent Possible!

THE WAYMAKER

In John's gospel, Jesus made seven declarations:

> I am the bread of life.
> I am the light of the world.
> I am the door.
> I am the vine.
> I am the good shepherd.
> I am the resurrection and the life.
> I am the way, the truth, and the life.[11]

Jesus is the Way, but He's more than that. Jesus is the Waymaker! Along with those seven declarations, John included seven signs performed by Jesus. Each one presents overwhelming evidence as to Jesus's identity as the Adjacent Possible.

Jesus was surrounded by five thousand hangry people when a little boy gave Him his lunch. That's great, but there's no way you feed five thousand people with five loaves and two fish. No way!

Way!

If you put what you have in your hands into the hands of the Way-maker, 5 plus 2 doesn't equal 7 anymore. 5 + 2 = 5,000 R12. You have more left over than you started with![12]

Jesus encountered a man born blind. If you're born blind, that means there are no synaptic connections between the optic nerve and the visual cortex of your brain. There is no way this man will ever have his vision restored. No way!

Way!

The Waymaker did synaptogenesis, installing new synaptic pathways in this blind man's brain![13]

Lazarus was four days dead. There was no way he would ever see the light of day again. No way!

Way!

The same voice that said "Let there be light" said "Lazarus, come forth."[14]

He is the God who makes sidewalks through the sea.[15]

He is the God who makes iron ax-heads float.[16]

He is the God who makes the sun stand still.[17]

I'm not sure who said it first, but we are an Easter people living in a Good Friday world. Our faith often looks foolish for a few days! It won't add up right away. It won't make sense at first. So, what do we do? We begin every day at the place where all things are possible and make a beeline for the empty tomb.

This is where we cut the rope!

SHADOW FUTURE

"The adjacent possible is a kind of shadow future," said Steven Johnson, "hovering on the edges of the present state of things."[18] We tend to see shadows in a negative light. Past-tense regret and future-tense anxiety can cast long shadows on the present, but that is when and where God overshadows us. His grace is sufficient. His power is made perfect in weakness. And He who began a good work will carry it to completion.[19]

Remember David versus Goliath?

No one saw David's potential, not even David's dad. All he saw was a shepherd, but David had a shadow future as the king of Israel. You are not the labels put on you by other people. You are who God says you are! You may not like the situation you find yourself in. Can I remind you of something? You may be in crisis, but you are in Christ. And that makes you more than a conqueror![20]

We live at the intersection of two theologies, two realities. God's faithfulness is pursuing us from the past, and God's sovereignty is bearing down on us from the future. Look back, and it's so far so God. Look ahead, and the best is yet to come.

What is your shadow future?

What are your adjacent possibilities?

That's a question only you can answer, but you will have to cut the rope. Faith is taking the first step before God reveals the second step. Isn't that what Elisha Otis did? He had no idea his invention would turn the world upside down. All he knew was that he needed to sell safety elevators to stay in business. Imagining unborn tomorrows doesn't mean figuring out every facet of your future. It's mustering the courage to take the next step!

> Faith is confidence in what we hope for and assurance about what we do not see.[21]

Faith is spelled a few ways, but one of them is *goals*. You won't accomplish 100 percent of the goals you don't set. Before setting them, make sure they glorify God. God won't honor the goals that don't honor Him. If you want to see my life goal list or download "Seven Steps to Setting Life Goals," visit markbatterson.com/wintheday.

How do you know whether a goal honors God? That's not an easy question to answer, but I'd start by checking your motives! In my experience, God-honoring goals are often God-sized goals. You can't accomplish them without God's help. That's how God gets the glory. He does things you can't take credit for!

THIS IS CRAZY

A few years ago, I hiked the Inca Trail to Machu Picchu. It ranks right behind the Grand Canyon in terms of difficulty. While we were there, Parker and I decided to check a life goal off our lists and go paragliding over the Sacred Valley.

That's one of those goals that sounds great on paper! I might add, at ground level. When you're staring at a cliff that drops ten thousand feet, you second-guess that goal. I must admit, a sixty-second orientation in Spanish did nothing to alleviate my fear of heights. Plus, my Peruvian tandem partner was a teenager who was half my height. All I remember him saying was "Run as fast as you can off the cliff, then lift your legs." That's all you've got? So I did what any good father would do. I let Parker go first.

As I sprinted toward that cliff, one thought was racing through my head: *This is crazy; this is crazy; this is crazy!* When I ran out of real estate, I lifted my legs, and an updraft caught our chute. The next thing I knew, I was sailing over the Sacred Valley and another thought was racing through my head: *This is awesome; this is awesome; this is awesome!*

I lost my lunch seven times, so it was less awesome for my tandem partner behind me. But I learned a lesson at ten thousand feet: *if you aren't willing to put yourself in "this is crazy" situations, you will never experience "this is awesome" moments.*

Imagining unborn tomorrows feels a little like running off that cliff. Some people will even call you crazy. So be it. Turning a crack house into Ebenezers Coffeehouse was crazy. We had no business going into the coffeehouse business, except for the fact that God had called us to do it. Did we make some mistakes along the way? Of course we did. You always do.

Since running off that cliff, we have served millions of customers and given away every penny of profit. Crazy turned into awesome! The key? Cutting the rope. Make sure God has given you the green light. If He has, it's go, set, ready!

Pull a Brodie

On July 23, 1886, a twenty-two-year-old daredevil named Steve Brodie jumped off the newly constructed Brooklyn Bridge. According to the *New York Times*, he made the 120-foot jump because of a $200 bet.[22] Brodie survived the jump, collected the money, and eventually starred in a Broadway play that recreated his infamous jump into the East River.

It's no longer a familiar phrase, but *pulling a Brodie* was once synonymous with a dangerous stunt, a calculated risk, a life-altering leap of faith. Not unlike paragliding over the Sacred Valley, it scares the living daylights out of you, but it's awesome *afterward*. Brodies don't always add up on paper, but they often prove to be the defining moments of our lives.

When I was nineteen years old, I walked into the admissions office at the University of Chicago and pulled a Brodie. I informed them that they could have their full-ride scholarship back. The U of C was the third-ranked university in the country that year, and I wasn't paying a penny for my education. I'll never forget the confused look on the face of the admissions counselor when I told her I was transferring to Central Bible College. She had a hard time transferring my credits because it wasn't even regionally accredited. That move made no sense academically or financially. It was a dangerous stunt but not as dangerous as rejecting what I believed to be God's plan and purpose for my life. I wasn't jumping on a $200 bet, but I had spotted my adjacent possible.

There are moments in life when playing it *safe* is *risky*! You've got to make the move, make the call, make the leap. And, I might add, make a mistake! Did I second-guess that decision to transfer? More than once! Did it involve a measure of sacrifice? A leap of faith always does. But—praise God—that leap is still paying dividends many decades later! Those are the moments that become milestones.

You are one decision away from a totally different life! It might be the hardest decision you ever make, but that is probably what will make it the best decision you ever make. Did you know that the Latin root of the word *decide* means "to cut"? It's time!

What rope do you need to cut?

What are you waiting for?

10

The Grand Gesture

*Quit living as if the purpose of life is to
arrive safely at death.*

In 1976, a professor at Northwestern University published a paper titled "Knee-Deep in the Big Muddy: A Study of Escalating Commitment to a Chosen Course of Action."[1] Dr. Barry Staw described a behavioral pattern called the escalation of commitment. It's the natural tendency, despite increasingly negative outcomes, to keep doing what you've been doing even when it obviously is not working!

Can I ask a question? How's that working for you?

I hate to be the bearer of bad news, but your actions are perfectly designed to achieve the results you're getting. Your relational behaviors are perfectly designed to achieve the relational results you're getting! Your health and wellness behaviors are perfectly designed to achieve the health and wellness results you're getting!

Isn't that a little harsh? What about people who are struggling with a debilitating disease caused by a genetic disorder? That is an important distinction to make. I'm certainly not suggesting that everything you face is your fault, but you still need to cut the rope. How? By making courageous decisions that chart a new course.

Your bad habits have got the best of you long enough. Enough is enough! And that goes for every self-defeating behavior! We all have triggers and tendencies that serve as trip wires. We've got to cut the rope by cutting those wires. How? The best way to break a bad habit is by establishing a good habit.

When you attempt to establish a new habit, initial progress is slow. In project management, it's called an S curve. It takes time to gain momentum. The first step is always the hardest, and the steps will get harder before they get easier! That's true of every good habit, isn't it? Start working out, and you get sore. Start tightening the belt on your budget, and it hits you where it hurts. Start dieting, and you crave sugar even more! Start praying, and your mind wanders all over tarnation. You've got to work hard to establish a new habit, and you've got to do so one day at a time.

That brings us back to this question: *Can you do it for a day?*

We need to imagine unborn tomorrows, not worry about them. It does no good worrying about next week, next month, or next year. As Jesus said, "Can any one of you by worrying add a single hour to your life?"[2]

CHANGE OF SCENERY

In 2007, author J. K. Rowling was struggling to finish the final novel, *The Deathly Hallows,* in her seven-part Harry Potter series. She was feeling stressed, trying to connect the dots in a way that would satisfy millions of Harry Potter fanatics. No pressure! Rowling tried writing the book in her home office, but she kept getting distracted. "There came a day," she said, "where the window cleaner came, the kids were at home, the dogs were barking."[3] She couldn't finish because she couldn't focus. What did Rowling do? She checked into the five-star Balmoral Hotel in downtown Edinburgh. Must be nice!

The change of scenery helped Rowling rediscover her writing flow, and the result was a Guinness World Record. *The Deathly Hallows* sold more than ten million copies within twenty-four hours of its release![4] "Rowling's decision to check into a luxurious hotel suite near Edinburgh Castle," said Georgetown professor Cal Newport, "is an example of a curious but effective strategy in the world of deep work: *the grand gesture.*"[5]

In one sense, this is nothing new. In fact, it's as old as building altars! When God wants to do a deep work within us, that deep work often necessitates a grand gesture. I would say that Noah's ark qualifies, wouldn't you? Go big or go home! Of course, grand gestures come in lots of shapes and sizes. The Israelites circled Jericho for seven days. Elisha burned his plowing equipment. Ezekiel lay on his left side for 390 days. The wise men followed a star all the way to Bethlehem. Peter and Andrew dropped their nets. And the Ephesians burned their sorcery scrolls in a giant bonfire.[6]

For the record, not every grand gesture is a good gesture. Pilate washed his hands in public right before turning Jesus over to a bloodthirsty mob. In his words, "I am not guilty of nor responsible for this righteous Man's blood."[7] The problem with that is this: *inaction is an action* and *indecision is a decision.* Pilate was response-able. It was within his power to defend an innocent man, but he played the coward.

Make sure your grand gesture is a good gesture!

I'm no J. K. Rowling. For starters, I write under my name, not my initials. But I do resonate with her strategy. I wrote my first book in much the same way she did. No, I didn't check into a five-star hotel. I turned a little greasy spoon, Bagels and Baguettes, into my writing room. Then I imposed my thirty-fifth birthday on myself as a deadline.

I felt called to write when I was twenty-two, but I had nothing to show for it thirteen years later. I had done a lot of reading but little writing. I came to despise my birthday because it was an annual reminder of a dream deferred. That's when I cut the rope. I gave myself a deadline; then I went to work on it one day at a time. I won the day, forty days in a row. The result was a self-published book, *ID: The True You.* Is it my best book? No, it is not. I tried to get it out of circulation, but once it's on Amazon, it's forever! I had, however, pulled a Brodie. I had proved to myself and to God that I could write a book.

Do you have a dream that is gathering dust? Give yourself a deadline! Not just to finish, but to start. You can't just imagine unborn tomorrows; you've got to get up every morning and move in the direction of that dream. Need a little more motivation? Delayed obedience is disobedience!

Simple Living

In March 1845, Henry David Thoreau received a letter from poet William Ellery Channing. "Build yourself a hut, & there begin the grand process of devouring yourself alive," wrote Channing. "I see no other alternative, no other hope for you."[8]

That challenge was the catalyst for a two-year experiment in simple living that began on July 4, 1845. Thoreau's grand gesture? Moving into a tiny home on a piece of property owned by Ralph Waldo Emerson. For the record, minimalism is a grand gesture, especially in a culture addicted to consumerism. The result was Thoreau's magnum opus, *Walden*. For two years, Thoreau communed with nature. His experiment went beyond deliberate practice. It was an all-inclusive rule of life. Let's call it deliberate living.

> I went to the woods because I wished to live deliberately, to front only the essential facts of life, and see if I could not learn what it had to teach, and not, when I came to die, discover that I had not lived.[9]

Most of us make this discovery too late in life! We live as if the purpose of life were to arrive safely at death. We take the path of least resistance. Henry David Thoreau died before Robert Frost was born, but Frost's admiration for Thoreau is well documented. One can't help but wonder whether Frost had Thoreau in mind when he penned "The Road Not Taken." One way or the other, Thoreau definitely chose the road less traveled.

Remember the formula? Deliberate Practice + Desirable Difficulty = Durable Learning.

We explored deliberate practice in part 1 and desirable difficulty in part 2. What is durable learning? The Latin source of the word *educate* means "to draw out." Based on the way we teach, you would think it means "to cram in." When you cram for finals, you are using rote memorization. That works for short-term memory and is generally good for grades but not great for imagining unborn tomorrows.

Durable learning goes beyond head knowledge. It's knowledge that has gone from your head to your heart to your gut. It's not an Ivy League or ivory tower education. It's the school of hard knocks. It's not facts; it's convictions. It's knowing that you know that you know. And the more you know, the more you know how much you don't know. It fuels what Albert Einstein called "a holy curiosity."[10] The reality? Most of us are educated way beyond the level of our obedience already. We don't need to know more. We need to *do more* with what we know. That's what cutting the rope is all about.

Elisha Otis may have known more about the mechanics of safety elevators than anyone on earth, but it would have made no difference if he had not acted on that knowledge. Doing is knowing, and knowing is doing. At the end of the day, God isn't going to say, "Well thought," "Well planned," or "Well intentioned." There is one commendation: "Well done, good and faithful servant!"[11]

Durable learning results in core convictions that become your rule of life—the thing that makes you tick, makes you tock. Your modus operandi. Your raison d'être. That rule of life encompasses the God-sized goals and the God-ordained passions that push you to become the best version of yourself possible.

TWO TOMORROWS

Benjamin Franklin said, "One to-day is worth two to-morrows."[12] In other words, *don't put off till tomorrow what can be done today*! Of course, most of us prefer Mark Twain's approach: "Never put off till to-morrow what you can do the day after to-morrow just as well."[13]

In his book *The Alphabet of Grace*, Frederick Buechner notes that every moment of every day is "gilded with goodbyes."[14] It may seem somber to say that you're experiencing everything for the last time, but this perspective makes every moment a holy moment. Once today is gone, you can't get it back. Today is the first day and last day of your life. Buechner explained, "It is the first day because it has never been before and the last day because it will never be again."[15]

If you want to win the day, you've got to live like it's the first day and last day of your life. I'll take it one step further. If you are in Christ, you no longer live! Isn't that what the apostle said? "I have been crucified with Christ and I no longer live, but Christ lives in me. The life I now live in the body, I live by faith in the Son of God."[16]

That doesn't mean you don't make long-range plans. Imagining un-born tomorrows is playing the long game, but it involves an immediacy that is quite different from urgency. Urgency is born of anxiety, while immediacy is born of faith. Faith is prophetic, but it's not presumptu-ous. Remember Walter Chrysler? Faith plans for tomorrow, but it doesn't take tomorrow for granted. It actually lives like there's no to-morrow. Buechner put it this way:

All the unkept promises if they are ever to be kept have to be kept today. All the unspoken words if you do not speak them today will never be spoken.[17]

We tend to fixate on sins of commission while ignoring sins of omis-sion. A sin of commission is doing something you should not have done. A sin of omission is a missed opportunity. The apostle James said in no uncertain terms, "Whoever knows the right thing to do and fails to do it, for him it is sin."[18] More specifically, a sin of omission.

Our greatest regrets at the end of our lives won't be the mistakes we made. They'll be the moments we missed because we were too busy or too lazy. They'll be the opportunities we left on the table because we were too scared or too distracted.

SEVEN CIRCLES

Gratitude is thanking God *after* He does it.

Faith is thanking God *before* He does it.

As we imagine unborn tomorrows, we have to recognize that everything is created twice. The first creation is spiritual. Prayer is the way we write history before it happens. It's the difference between *letting things happen* and *making things happen.* How God answers our prayers is up to Him, but we need to pray through till the breakthrough.

In August 1996, I felt prompted to pray a perimeter around Capitol Hill. I was reading Joshua 1:3: "I will give you every place where you set your foot." I felt like God wanted me to stake claim to that promise, so I prayed a 4.7-mile circle around the Hill. Two decades later, we own six properties on that prayer circle with a combined value of more than $75 million. Did I mention that we own them debt-free? Only God. There is no way I could have orchestrated that many miracles. I didn't think of it as a grand gesture at the time, but that's exactly what it was.

> The gates of Jericho were securely barred because of the Israelites. No one went out and no one came in.
>
> Then the LORD said to Joshua, "See, I have delivered Jericho into your hands."[19]

Did you catch the verb tense? It should be future tense: "I will deliver." It hadn't happened yet, right? So, why is it past tense: "I have delivered"? Because every miracle happens twice! The breakthrough always happens in the spiritual realm first. Then—and only then—does it manifest itself in the physical realm. God had already delivered Jericho in the spiritual realm; all the Israelites had to do was keep circling for seven days.

Before feeding the five thousand, Jesus asked Philip a question: "Where are we to buy bread, so that all these people may eat?"[20] Do you really think Jesus was asking Philip to GPS the nearest Panera Bread? Me neither! Jesus was kneading him. How do we know this? Because Scripture says, "He well knew what He was about to do."[21]

Take a deep breath! God's got this! God wants us to get where He wants us to go more than we want to get there, and He's awfully good at getting us there.

There is one catch, of course. None of us know how long it will take! As my friend T. L. Rogers said, "It would be a lot easier if God told us how long." One of the most poignant questions in Psalms is this one: "How long, O Lord?"[22] We're like little children in the back seat putting this question on repeat: *When will we get there?* God's answer is a lot like ours as parents: *One minute less than the last time you asked.*

My advice? Keep circling Jericho!

Same Day Delivery

There is a sin of presumption—*getting ahead of God.*

There is also a sin of procrastination—*falling behind.*

Imagining unborn tomorrows avoids both extremes. Yes, we need to do things that will make a difference a hundred years from now. But like everything else, the long game is played one day at a time!

According to Deuteronomic law, "Pay [the hired workers] their wages each day before sunset, because they are poor and are counting on it."[23] What does that mean? Pay your pledge before it's due! The law demanded same day delivery long before Amazon Prime.

Here's a thought: leverage the sunset as a daily deadline. Isn't that what the ancient Israelites did?

When Abraham was ninety-nine, God confirmed His covenant one last time. Any guess how He did so? With a grand gesture, of course! This one makes Abraham's long walk look like a cakewalk. As a token of the covenant, God told Abraham to circumcise every male member of his household. I won't detail what that involves, but when it comes to outpatient surgery, most people want a day or two to think it over. Scripture is explicit about the timing of Abraham's obedience: "On the very same day Abraham was circumcised."[24]

What day? "The very same day." The longer you wait, the harder it gets! Hard decisions only get harder. In this instance, harder is *not* better!

Every time I go after a goal—whether it's writing a book, training for a triathlon, or starting a business—I am absolutely overwhelmed at the outset. The finish line looks so far away that it's hard to even get started. I have to fight against feelings of doubt and discouragement. The hardest day to win, hands down, is day one! That's why you need to give yourself a start date. After all, *you cannot finish what you do not start.*

Here is a lesson I've learned the hard way: *whatever you don't do today, you are less likely to do tomorrow!* You don't feel like dieting today? You'll feel less like dieting tomorrow. Don't put off till tomorrow what you can do today!

Today, if you hear his voice,
do not harden your hearts.[25]

Like Moses, the writer of Hebrews advocated same day delivery. If you don't do it today, your heart becomes a little harder. So does your hearing. Before you know it, it's difficult to discern the promptings of the Holy Spirit.

According to Parkinson's Law, the amount of time it takes to accomplish a task depends on the time allotted. The time it takes expands or contracts based on deadlines. If you have two days, it'll take two days. If you have two weeks, it'll take two weeks. If you have two months, it'll take two months. I almost always hit my writing deadlines—but not a day too soon! Part of it is my perfectionism. Part of it is human nature.

Remember this seven-word question: *Can you do it for a day?* Let me add a little immediacy. Today is the day! If you wait until you're ready, you'll be waiting the rest of your life.

Cut the rope!

Habit 6—Wind the Clock

Time is measured in minutes;
life is measured in moments.

A mong the oldest pieces of art in the United States Capitol is the *Car of History* clock that greets guests as they enter Statuary Hall. Above the clock stands Clio, the Muse of history. She holds a book, in which she records events as they unfold. The sculpture was created by Carlo Franzoni, and the clockwork was made and installed by eighty-four-year-old Simon Willard in 1837.

During a speech before a joint session of Congress, historian and Pulitzer Prize–winner David McCullough pointed to Willard's clock as an important object lesson: "It is . . . a clock with two hands and an old-fashioned face, the kind that shows what time it is now, what time it used to be . . . and what time it will become."[1]

Past, present, and future.

That's how we divide time, and David McCullough is right: a right relationship with those three time zones is critically important. You've got to bury dead yesterdays and imagine unborn tomorrows if you want to win the day. But please note that time, as we know it, is nothing more than a human construct. Sure, God is the one who named night and day and divided time into weeks and months and years. But God does not exist within the four dimensions of space-time He created. "With the Lord a day is like a thousand years, and a thousand years are like a day."[2]

The arrow of time moves in one direction for us, but God is omnipresent. What does that mean?

God is *here, there,* and *everywhere!*

God is present *yesterday, today,* and *tomorrow.*

Time management is painfully practical, and we'll certainly wind the clock that way. But the theological underpinnings of time are imperative to understand. Did you know that God is preparing good works in advance for you?[3] That He is ordering your footsteps?[4] He is in the business of strategically positioning you in the right place at the right time. Simply put, God is setting you up! The unborn tomorrows you imagine were sovereignly prepared by God Himself before the creation of the world.

I like John Piper's take on time in his brilliantly titled book *Don't Waste Your Life.* He warned against "chronological snobbery," a concept he borrowed from C. S. Lewis.

> Newness is no virtue and oldness is no vice. Truth and beauty and goodness are not determined by when they exist. Nothing is inferior for being old, and nothing is valuable for being modern. This has freed me from the tyranny of novelty and opened for me the wisdom of the ages.[5]

Let me double back to historian David McCullough. "I have decided that the digital watch is the perfect symbol of an imbalance in outlook in our day," he said in that same speech before Congress. "It tells us only what time it is now, at this instant, as if that were all anyone would wish or need to know."[6]

The imbalanced outlook McCullough alluded to takes many forms, from busyness to laziness. It's the impetus for hurry. It's the recipe for regret. A right relationship with time means recognizing, first and foremost, that time is measured in *minutes* but life is measured in *moments!* Not all time is created equal. As Albert Einstein so ably demonstrated, time is relative.

The sixth habit—*wind the clock*—stewards time in two ways. It makes the most of every minute, but it also makes the most of every moment. It's acutely aware of everything that is happening right here, right now. It also keeps a constant eye on eternity. Most importantly, it doesn't lose faith in the end of the story.

The ancient Greeks had two words for time—*chronos* and *kairos*. They are two sides of the same coin, but they are as different as heads and tails. Chronos is clock time, as in Willard's clock. We get our word *chronology* from *chronos*. Chronos is sequential—past, present, future. Chronos is quantitative—it counts seconds, minutes, and hours. Managing chronos time is incredibly important. If you don't control your calendar, your calendar will control you. But it's not as important as "redeeming the time,"[7] which is where kairos enters the equation.

Kairos makes the most of every opportunity. It's the sixth sense that perceives the promptings of the Holy Spirit. Kairos doesn't keep time as much as it makes time. When it discerns a holy moment, it takes off its shoes. The poet Elizabeth Barrett Browning said it this way:

> Earth's crammed with heaven,
> And every common bush afire with God:
> But only he who sees, takes off his shoes,
> the rest sit round it, and pluck blackberries.[8]

I believe in Lombardi time. If you aren't fifteen minutes early, you're late. But the greatest moments in life are off the clock, off the grid. Chronos is all about making good time. Kairos is about enjoying the journey. It's about smelling the roses. It's less about getting to a particular destination in record time and more about who you become along the way. We'll wind both the chronos and the kairos clocks with the sixth habit, but we'll focus more time and energy on kairos because it comes less naturally.

It's time to wind the clock!

11

Counterclockwise

Show me the size of your dream,
and I'll show you the size of your God.

In 1905, Albert Einstein did a thought experiment that would ultimately win him a Nobel Prize. Imagine two twins. One of them gets
on a spacecraft traveling four-fifths the speed of light and returns to
Earth ten years later. When the twins are reunited, they will be different
ages. The earthbound twin will be ten years older, while the interstellar
twin will be six years older.[1] How is this possible? The faster we travel,
the slower time moves.

At half the speed of light, time is slowed by 13 percent. At 99 percent
the speed of light, it is seven times slower—one minute is reduced to 8.5
seconds! Simply put, time is relative. We move too slowly to notice it in
real life, but the technical term is time dilation.

Remember Tony Campolo and his top-of-the-Empire-State-Building
moment? Or my bottom-of-the-Grand-Canyon moment? Time stood
still. Why? It was a kairos moment. Our job is to enjoy those moments!
If we don't, life passes us by. Isn't that what the ancient psalmist said?

This is the day that the LORD has made;
let us rejoice and be glad in it.[2]

Winding the clock is recognizing every moment for what it is—a gift
from God. The challenge, of course, is that we are as easily distracted as

Dug, the talking dog in the movie *Up*. *Squirrel!* It doesn't help that life is coming at us faster than ever!

The digital universe of data doubles in size every two years and has now reached forty-four zettabytes.[3] I have no idea what that even means, but I think it translates to "information overload." We are bombarded by at least five thousand advertisements every day. According to time management experts, the average person gets interrupted every eight minutes.[4] If you have young children, eight minutes would feel like an eternity! Right? The average person spends two hours and twenty-two minutes on social media per day.[5] And I would be willing to bet that the pace of life isn't slowing down anytime soon!

Sociologists have a name for this frenetic pace of life: *urban metabolism*. Studies have found a correlation between size of city and pace of life—the bigger the city, the faster we walk. Every day, we're shuffling, shuffling.[6]

Is it fair to say that our lives are moving a little too fast?

"When I pronounce the word Future," said Polish poet Wisława Szymborska, "the first syllable already belongs to the past."[7] The poet Robert Herrick said it this way in his poem "Make Much of Time":

> *Gather ye rose-buds while ye may,*
> *Old Time is still a-flying;*
> *And this same flower that smiles today*
> *Tomorrow will be dying.*"[8]

Old time is still a-flying—faster than ever! But what if there were a way to wind the clock and slow it down?

NEOTENY

In 1979, Harvard professor Ellen Langer orchestrated an unorthodox experiment dubbed "the counterclockwise study." Langer's hypothesis was based on a mind-over-matter hunch: "If we could turn back the clock psychologically, could we also turn it back physically?"[9]

Chronologically, we all age at the same rate. We get one day older every day. Psychologically, we all age at different rates and in different ways! We all know people who are the same age chronologically, but you would never know it by the way they look, act, or think. We say that time has been kind to some and unkind to others, but are there factors we can control when it comes to aging well?

Langer recruited participants in their late seventies or early eighties, pitching her study as research on reminiscing. She knew she couldn't turn back time, but she could turn back the clock. "We would re-create the world of 1959 and ask subjects to live as though it were twenty years earlier. If we put the mind back twenty years, would the body reflect this change?"[10]

Langer and her team retrofitted an old monastery in Peterborough, New Hampshire, to recreate 1959. When participants walked through the front door, it was like stepping back in time. A vintage radio played Perry Como. *The Ed Sullivan Show* was rebroadcast on a black-and-white television. Books and magazines were curated to conjure 1959. Even the mirrors, which would have reminded participants of their actual ages, were removed. To help participants get into character, they were also asked to write brief autobiographies as though it were 1959 and send photographs of their younger selves.

The group was given a ground rule: no one was allowed to discuss anything that happened after 1959. They discussed historical events as if they were current events. Talking *past tense* was out of bounds. Everything was experienced *present tense,* as if it were happening in real time.[11] It was a total time warp.

Before I share the results of Langer's study, let me share one of my favorite words—*neoteny.* It's a zoological term that refers to the retention of youthful qualities into adulthood. I'm not sure who comes to mind for you, but I immediately think of Caleb. Biblically speaking, he's the patron saint of neoteny. When he finally stepped foot in the Promised Land after forty years of wandering in the wilderness, he was not unlike this group of geriatrics who stepped into the retrofitted monastery. Caleb felt forty all over again!

I am as strong today as I was the day Moses sent me; as my strength was then, so is my strength now.[12]

I know this is Caleb's self-assessment, but I have no reason to doubt him. I think he could deadlift as much at eighty-five as he could at forty. How? I have a theory, but let me have a little fun first. Caleb was the original Chuck Norris! I can only imagine the jokes that circulated the ancient internet.

Caleb counted to infinity—twice.

Death once had a near-Caleb experience.

When Alexander Graham Bell invented the telephone, he had a missed call from Caleb.

When Caleb fell in water, he didn't get wet. The water got Caleb.

Caleb didn't wear a watch; he simply decided what time it was.

I could keep going, but I'll stop there. My theory? As long as you're going after a God-sized dream with God-given passion, you're never past your prime! Vision makes time fly, but it slows down the aging process.

MIND OVER MATTER

Before the counterclockwise study began, participants were tested for a wide variety of biological and intellectual markers. Just one week after turning back time to 1959, the participants showed measurable improvement in physical strength, manual dexterity, and taste sensitivity.

Their hearing and vision improved, as did their performance on intelligence tests. Even their fingers lengthened as the effects of arthritis diminished.[13]

On the first day of the study, some of these geriatrics could barely shuffle through the front door. On the last day of the study, they went outside and played an impromptu game of football on the front lawn.[14] It was touch, not tackle, but impressive nonetheless. Too bad they didn't have pay-per-view back then!

The participants weren't the only ones who felt like time had been turned back. An independent group of volunteers who knew nothing of the counterclockwise study were asked to evaluate *before* and *after* pictures of the participants. The *after* photos were judged to be more than two years younger than the *before* photos! And that was after only one week.

Let me add one more fascinating footnote.

Before initiating the counterclockwise study, Ellen Langer consulted with geriatricians to determine the biological markers of age. She was told that there were none! Doctors discern age the same way the rest of us do—by birth date. Beyond that, science cannot pinpoint someone's age through a physical examination or blood test.

"I have come to believe less and less that biology is destiny," contends Ellen Langer. "If a group of elderly adults could produce such dramatic changes in their lives, so too can the rest of us."[15] How? Wind the clock!

PREDECISIONS

Part of my fascination with the counterclockwise study has to do with my goal of celebrating my one hundredth birthday. I'm probably not a prime candidate to become a centenarian, given my medical history. I suffered from severe asthma for forty years. I've had half a dozen knee surgeries. And I have a foot less intestines than the average person after emergency surgery for ruptured intestines. That said, I'm imagining lots of unborn tomorrows. I want a cake with one hundred candles, and

I'll try to blow them out with one breath. I know there are lots of factors I cannot control, but I'm trying to control the ones I can. And that starts with my mindset.

Aging, like everything else, is mind over matter! Ellen Langer would say it's *mindfulness over matter*! Mindfulness is paying attention to the present moment, and it's one way we wind the clock. It's acute awareness of what we're thinking, what we're feeling. And, I might add, awareness of what the Spirit of God is doing in us and around us. This goes beyond Langer's definition, but mindfulness is the mind of Christ. It's living in sync with God's Spirit. It's keeping one eye on eternity and the other eye on opportunity. Simply put, it's making the most of every moment.

Remember the ground rule for Langer's study? Participants were not allowed to talk *past tense*. Everything was experienced *present tense*. This is easier said than done, but it's the only way to win the day. Mindfulness is living present tense, like the participants in the study.

According to Ellen Langer, mindfulness is premeditated cognitive commitments. It's the predecisions we make every day, like *eating the frog*. King Solomon said it this way: "As [a man] thinketh in his heart, so is he."[16] If the battle is won or lost in the mind, predecisions are the way we wage war. It's making decisions *before* you have to make the decision.

Can I give you a classic example? After being sold into slavery, Joseph went to work for a man named Potiphar. Potiphar's wife did everything she could to seduce Joseph. How often? Every. Single. Day. "She kept putting pressure on Joseph day after day, but he refused to sleep with her, and he kept out of her way as much as possible."[17]

If you wait to make a decision until you find yourself in a tempting situation, good luck with that. That's how we make bad decisions.

Joseph didn't make a decision in the heat of the moment when faced with constant flirtation. He made a predecision not to sleep with a woman who was not his wife. Case closed. You've got to establish boundaries, then put up a No Trespassing sign.

Joseph would eventually save two nations from famine, but that opportunity wouldn't have presented itself if he hadn't made a good predecision many years before. His premeditated cognitive commitment? Joseph "kept out of her way as much as possible." That's a good rule of thumb when it comes to temptation. You've got to avoid it at every turn. I don't know what tempts you, but I wouldn't touch it with a ten-foot pole!

THE POWER OF SUGGESTION

More than a hundred years ago, a British psychiatrist named J. A. Hadfield did a fascinating study on the power of suggestion. Using a dynamometer that measured grip strength, Hadfield tested the effect of suggestion on physical strength. He told the participants to grip the dynamometer with all their strength. Their average output was 101 pounds of pressure under normal conditions. Hadfield then put his subjects under the power of suggestion and told them that they were very weak. Their grip strength decreased to twenty-nine pounds—less than one-third their normal strength. One of the test subjects, who happened to be a prizefighter, said that his arm felt tiny, like a baby's! The subjects were tested a third time and told that they were very strong. The average grip strength skyrocketed to 142 pounds.[18]

Remember the first habit—*flip the script*? We've got to remember right, and that requires historical revisionism. Da Vinci called it post-imagining, which is postediting. It's a more graceful, more truthful rewriting of our stories. Why is it so important? In the words of Dr. Joseph Dispenza, "The brain does not know the difference between what it sees and what it remembers."[19] It's time to add *imagination* to the mix. The brain does not differentiate between what it sees and what it imagines either. Remember the *Australia II* and the audiotape they put on repeat? Before they even set sail, they had won the race 2,190 times in their minds! That kind of *preimagining* has profound implications and applications when it comes to imagining unborn tomorrows.

For the love of friends and family, own your age. Everyone knows you're not twenty-nine! Owning your age is celebrating the compound interest of long obedience in the same direction. Acting your age is a different thing, and I advise against it. Acting your age is how we get old. We let age dictate what we can do. Age is not an excuse God allows—just ask Abraham and Sarah.

In many respects, age is a self-fulfilling prophecy. Don't tell people you're twenty-nine if you're not, but it's okay to *think* and *act* like you're twenty-nine. Your body may know the difference, but your brain does not.

It's never too late to be who you might have been. You cut the rope by cutting the rope. You wind the clock by cutting the rug!

Our family celebrated a few weddings this past year, and my mom dominated the dance floor! I won't reveal her age, even though she wouldn't care if I did. Let's just say that people half her age had to take a break while she partied like it was 1999. After one of those weddings, I asked her how she does it. My mom seemed as surprised by my question as I was by her answer: "I stretch every day!" There you have it. I'm pretty sure she would have scored a touchdown or two in that geriatric game of touch football I mentioned!

Die Young

Ashley Montagu, the British American anthropologist, said, "I want to die young at a ripe old age." I do too! For the record, Montagu lived to the ripe old age of ninety-four. I love old souls who have wisdom beyond their years, but I also love octogenarians who are young at heart.

The idea of dying young at a ripe old age is a pretty good paraphrase of something Jesus said: "Unless you change and become like little children, you will never enter the kingdom of heaven."[20] To become like Christ is to become like a little child. The implications and applications of this one statement are kaleidoscopic, but it refers to approaching life with childlike humility, childlike wonder, childlike faith. You need to stay in touch with your inner child, no matter how old you get. To do that, you've got to ignore your inner critic!

We may be living longer than our ancestors, but they were better at aging. These days, aging is seen as an evil to be avoided at all costs, including the cost of cosmetic surgery. If looking younger makes you feel younger, so be it. But aging has a lot less to do with your appearance and a lot more to do with your attitude!

In his bestselling book *Tuesdays with Morrie*, Mitch Albom told about reconnecting with Morrie Schwartz, his college professor who was dying of Lou Gehrig's disease. Morrie shared lots of lessons that life had taught him, but my favorite is on the subject of aging. I appreciate his straightforward approach: "I *embrace* aging."[21]

Can we stop calling forty the new thirty, fifty the new forty, and sixty the new fifty? Where will it end? Let's call it what it is: forty is forty, fifty is fifty, and sixty is sixty! When it comes to aging, I believe in *name it, claim it*. You've earned your age! Quit discounting yourself by docking your age!

On their seventh Tuesday together, Morrie flipped the script on aging: "Aging is not just decay, you know. It's growth. It's more than the negative that you're going to die, it's also the positive that you *understand* you're going to die, and that you live a better life because of it."[22] The process of personal development never ends. I'm not who I was yesterday. I'm not who I will be tomorrow. I am a work in progress. The good news? It's never too late to be who I might have been. To that end, Morrie Schwartz shared one more profound perspective on aging:

> The truth is, part of me is every age. I'm a three-year-old, I'm a five-year-old, I'm a thirty-seven-year-old, I'm a fifty-year-old. I've been through all of them, and I know what it's like. I delight in being a child when it's appropriate to be a child. I delight in being a wise old man when it's appropriate to be a wise old man. Think of all I can be! I am every age, up to my own.[23]

Something about that is so liberating, isn't it? You are every age up to your own. Like with your past, you have to own your age or it will own you!

THE TWO-HUNDRED-YEAR PRESENT

Caleb was forty years old when he was chosen as one of twelve spies to do reconnaissance in the Promised Land. It was Caleb who cast vision to the nation: "Let us go up at once and possess it; we are well able to conquer it."[24] If I had to guess Caleb's StrengthsFinder profile, it would definitely include Positivity. Unfortunately, the negativity of the majority cost the Israelites forty years in the wilderness.

According to one rabbinic tradition, Caleb left the other spies after entering the Promised Land and paid a visit to Hebron. This was where the matriarch and patriarch, Sarah and Abraham, were buried. This was where they had built altars, pitched tents, and dug wells. Hebron was holy ground, and while I can't prove this, I can't help but wonder whether Caleb swore on his ancestors' graves that he would be back to reclaim what was rightfully theirs.

Fast-forward forty-five years, and Caleb was still winding the clock with vision. His entire adult life had been aimed at this singular goal, and it was almost within reach. You can feel the conviction in his voice, can't you? "Now give me this hill country."[25] Caleb possessed his piece of the Promised Land. Mission accomplished, right? Not so fast.

We think right here, right now. God is thinking nations and generations! Caleb wasn't conquering Hebron just for himself. More than four hundred years later, David would be crowned king in the city Caleb conquered. David was standing on Caleb's shoulders! It was Caleb's victory that made David's coronation possible! When you wind the clock the way Caleb did, your brave becomes someone else's breakthrough!

Sociologist Elise Boulding once diagnosed modern society with "temporal exhaustion." Sounds about right, doesn't it? She said, "If one is mentally out of breath all the time from dealing with the present, there is no energy left for imagining the future."[26] The solution? If you're going to dream big, you've got to think long. How long? Boulding recommended what she called "the 200-year present." It begins one hundred years ago, with those who have reached their one hundredth birthday. It ends with those born today who will live to be one hundred.

> By thinking about that span of time as encompassing the living present reality of people you know and care about, that span of time becomes accessible. It becomes our time in a very profound sense. This 200-year span belongs to us: it's our life space. It's the space in which we should be thinking, planning and making judgments, evaluating, hoping and dreaming.[27]

We are the beneficiaries of sacrifices we cannot imagine and risks we cannot calculate. We live in cities we did not build, drink from wells we did not dig, and harvest fields we did not plant. Why? Because people long, long ago wound the clock with their faith, hope, and love.

We are the answers to prayers we know nothing about. Why not return the favor? Quit wasting time, and wind the clock for the third and fourth generation. Go, set, ready!

12

Persistence Hunting

There is no finish line.

In 1973, a pair of Harvard scientists stuck a rectal thermometer in a cheetah's bum and somehow got it to run on a treadmill in their research lab.[1] You read that right. It's hard to imagine, but hold that thought.

In the late nineteenth century, an American army lieutenant turned explorer named Frederick Schwatka led an expedition through Mexico, where he encountered a remote tribe that lived off the land, off the grid. The Tarahumara made their homes in caves in the canyons of the Sierra Madre region of northern Mexico. In his recollections of this isolated tribe, Schwatka noted the unique running ability of the Tarahumara:

> In the depth of winter, with snow on the ground, the Tarahu-
> mari hunter, with nothing on but his rawhide sandals and a
> breech-clout, will start in pursuit of a deer and run it down after
> a chase of hours in length, the thin crust of snow impeding the
> animal so that it finally succumbs to its persistent enemy.[2]

Note the word *persistent* because the Tarahumara function as a pretty good definition. They would not be outrun, even by a wild animal. The original name of this ancient tribe, Rarámuri, literally means "the running people."[3] "Their fondness for extensive foot contests" is legendary![4]

They were running ultramarathons long before the Barkley Marathons. In 1867, eight Tarahumara women competed in a hundred-mile race. The winner finished in 13:25. Even more impressive? One of the women who finished the race had given birth ten days earlier![5]

In his 1893 memoir, *In the Land of Cave and Cliff Dwellers*, Schwatka said, "If night overtakes the pursuers they sleep on the trail, and resume the chase as early next morning as the light will allow."[6] This ancient hunting technique has a name: *persistence hunting*. Humans are slower than much of the rest of the animal kingdom, but we have one distinct advantage—sweat glands. The sixth habit—wind the clock—revolves around imagination, and when you combine it with perspiration, you can chase down just about anything!

Few of us hunt for food, but what if we pursued our dreams with Tarahumara-like persistence? Goal setting is persistence hunting. Go ahead and get some small wins under your belt while going after God-sized goals. It builds confidence and creates momentum. It's one way you fly the kite. But you should also set some stretch goals that will take a lifetime to accomplish. That's how you wind the clock.

SWEAT EQUITY

I haven't forgotten about the cheetah with the rectal thermometer, I promise you. Before sharing the results of that unique research, let me share actor Will Smith's not-so-secret secret to success:

> I'm not afraid to die on a treadmill. I will not be outworked. Period. You might have more talent than me. You might be smarter than me. You might be sexier than me. . . . But if we get on the treadmill together, there's two things—you're getting off first or I'm going to die.[7]

You know what I would pay to see? Will Smith versus the cheetah. A cheetah can run faster than a human—that's for sure. But once its body overheats, it has to stop. Wild animals like the cheetah can run fast, but they can't run continuously. Remember our unique advantage over the rest of the animal kingdom? I've already tipped the trump card—sweat glands. Well, that and the nuchal ligament that stabilizes your head while you run. If you're hunting wild game, or tracking down a fly ball in right field, it comes in awfully handy!

When was the last time you thanked God for sweat glands? Probably never. Sweat glands give us the ability to perspire, which enables us to run long distances without stopping. We can't outrun wild animals, but we can outlast them. How? We regulate body temperature better! I'm not sure we needed a cheetah's rectal thermometer to prove that, but science sure is fun!

The ancient art of persistence hunting is still being practiced by the Bushmen of the Kalahari Desert. An anthropologist named Louis Liebenberg once shadowed them on one of their hunts. They walked twenty miles before spotting a clutch of kudus, a very agile antelope. When they started running, Louis had his doubts: "No way these guys were going to catch one of those kudus on foot. No way."[8] Way! After isolating one of the kudus, they kept it running and kept it from getting shade. I won't tell you exactly how it ended, but a five-hundred-pound kudu can provide enough meat for an entire village for quite some time.

Persistence hunting is about ruthless efficiency. You can't waste energy. You can't waste time. You can't waste water. The same is true when you go after any God-sized goal. You've got to remain open minded while having a one-track mind. You've got to know your lane, then stay in it. Why? Slow and steady wins the race! It's survival of the persistent.

Front-Page News

I'll never forget August 12, 2001—it's one of those days that changed every day thereafter. We were five years into our church plant—five *long* years! It took five years for us to grow from our original core group of nineteen to an average attendance of 250. It took almost that long to become self-supporting, and even then, we were living offering to offering.

Many years later, National Community Church (NCC) would be recognized as one of the most innovative and influential churches in America. I promise you, it was not always that way! Yes, we planted the church in the shadow of the Capitol. But the key word is *shadow*. We did what we did in relative obscurity. There was nothing glamorous about our early days!

Then one day, a religion reporter from the *Washington Post* requested an interview. She had heard about our unique demographics—NCC was 80 percent single twentysomethings at the time—and she found that newsworthy. After the interview, she told me to keep an eye on the weekend religion section. The following Sunday, I walked into Union Station, where we were meeting at the time, and picked up a paper at the newsstand. I flipped to the religion section, and we weren't in it. Total disappointment. I folded the paper back up because if we weren't in it, I wasn't going to buy a $1.50 newspaper! That's when I saw it. The article about NCC made the front page of the *Washington Post,* Sunday edition.

I used to joke that it must have been a slow news day; then I felt convicted by the Holy Spirit. It wasn't a slow news day. It was God's time! It was God's favor! That front-page article was God's way of putting us on the map. We doubled in size that year, and we never looked back.

When I say that God is able to do more in one day than we can accomplish in a thousand lifetimes, I think of specific days like August 12, 2001. God showed up and showed off His favor! That said, it was preceded by lots of blood, sweat, and tears! You pray like it depends on God. But you also have to attack each day like it depends on you. That's how we wind the clock, and winding the clock takes lots of different forms.

For David, it was faithfully shepherding his sheep.

For Daniel, it was fasting from the king's food.

For Nehemiah, it was service with a smile.

For Benaiah, it was chasing a lion into a pit on a snowy day.

Like each of the seven habits, winding the clock is as unique as you are. But the best example may be the disciples gathering in an upper room to pray for ten days. They kept winding the clock each day. They had no idea that the Day of Pentecost would be the day that changed every day thereafter. None of us do! They were counting up, but I think God was counting down! Either way, nothing winds the clock like prayer.

One Day

There is a two-word phrase in Scripture that gives me goose bumps: "one day." Why? Because today could be the day! That phrase fuels my holy confidence with holy adrenaline! If we do the right thing day in and day out, God is going to show up and show off. There's going to be a tipping point. There's going to be a turning point. I can't tell you *when* or *where* or *how*, but it'll happen sooner or later! And that's true, even if it happens in eternity.

One day, Jonathan said to his armor-bearer, "Perhaps the LORD will act in our behalf."[9] One act of courage turned the tide against an archenemy. *One day,* Mordecai overheard an assassination plot while on duty at the king's gate.[10] That discovery turned the tables, and Mordecai became a key part of saving the Jewish people from genocide. *One day,* around three o'clock in the afternoon, Cornelius had a vision from God that turned history on a dime.[11]

Can I remind you of something? The stories we read in *minutes* took *years*! Abraham waited twenty-five years for God to fulfill His promise. Joseph's life went from bad to worse for thirteen years. Even Jesus didn't do any miracles until the age of thirty.

Don't envy other people's success if you aren't willing to emulate their work ethic. When it comes to success, we read the CliffsNotes. Yes, successful people have a way of making it look easier than it really is. But you and I both know how they got there. They ate more frogs and flew more kites than the rest of us, and they kept winding the clock day in and day out.

You hit your target weight one pound at a time.

You get debt-free one dollar at a time.

You get into shape one workout at a time.

You get your degree one class at a time.

You record the album one rehearsal at a time.

You win the game one practice at a time.

Imagining unborn tomorrows isn't just plotting the far-distant future. It's plodding one day at a time. It's putting one foot in front of the other when you don't feel like doing so. Life goals have to translate into daily habits! You have to wind the clock on your dreams every day.

FANATICAL CONSISTENCY

There is an old adage: "Rome wasn't built in a day." It's attributed to an English playwright a lot less famous than William Shakespeare—John Heywood. He's actually credited with quite a few idioms including "Out of sight, out of mind," "Better late than never," and "Many hands make light work."[12] Few things can be done in a day, but nothing can be done yesterday or tomorrow. Today is all we've got, so we'd better make it count.

When it comes to success, most of us aren't good at self-assessment. The same goes for failure. In one study of successful leaders, those leaders were at a loss when it came to pinpointing the cause of their success. They could point to "no single defining action, no grand program, no one killer innovation, no solitary lucky break, no wrenching revolution." The key? To quote one of those leaders, "Fanatical consistency."[13] In other words, keep winding the clock day after day.

Can I offer two pieces of advice?

First, don't get too discouraged if your dream takes a lot longer than originally planned. Maybe God is doing something bigger and better than you originally imagined! In the words of Oswald Chambers,

"God's aim looks like missing the mark because we are too short-sighted to see what He is aiming at."[14]

Second, don't call it quits unless you are released by God. If we had quit on National Community Church in the first five years, that decision would have affected only a few hundred people. Honestly, they could have found a more mature church to attend. But that's where imagining unborn tomorrows comes into play. The reality? We would have been quitting on everything God would do in and through National Community over the next two decades. We would have forfeited the hundreds of mission trips we've taken, the thousands of lives we've affected, and the millions of dollars we've given to kingdom causes.

COUNT THE DAYS

During the 2019 NCAA tournament, I did a chapel for the Virginia Tech Hokies before their Sweet Sixteen matchup with the Duke Blue Devils. It was their first Sweet Sixteen appearance in fifty-two years. I had known their coach at the time, Buzz Williams, since his coaching days at Marquette, so I was well aware of his penchant for daily discipline.

I had no idea, however, that it would be Buzz's last game as coach of the Hokies. I don't think he did either, but Buzz made every day count. How? By counting the days, quite literally! The day of that Sweet Sixteen matchup, Buzz mentioned that it was day 1,811 in his tenure as head coach of the Hokies. Does that strike you the way it strikes me? Do you know how many days you've worked your current job? I took note, in part, because I count the days since God healed my asthma.

I knew Buzz was a poster child for winning the day, but that might make him a patron saint. Who counts the number of days he's coached a team? I'll tell you who—someone who is making the most of them! If you want every day to count, count the days. If you don't count them, they actually count against you.

How seriously does God take a day? The answer is found in Numbers. Remember, the trip from Mount Sinai to the Promised Land was supposed to take only eleven days! So, why did it take forty years? The short answer is the Israelites' lack of faith, but the reason behind this length of time is a little more nuanced than that. The forty-year sentence was punishment for the forty days the spies spent in the Promised Land—one year for each day.[15]

In that equation, a day is worth a year. The psalmist upped the ante: "Better is one day in your courts than a thousand elsewhere."[16] The ratio is a thousand to one. The apostle Peter upped the ante again: "With the Lord a day is like a thousand years."[17]

The bottom line? Don't devalue the power of twenty-four hours! There is no standing still in God's kingdom. Either we're gaining ground or we're losing it. Whatever we don't count, we discount. If you don't win the day, guess what? You lose the day!

GET BETTER

After I spoke to his Hokies, Buzz invited me to stick around for their pregame meeting. The coaches and players watched film, which I expected. What I did not expect was a mindfulness exercise that would have made Ellen Langer proud. It would be best described as guided meditation. All that was missing was yoga mats and meditation music!

Buzz asked his players to pull out their journals; then he peppered them with thought-provoking questions: "What did you learn from your last game?" "What do you want to remember ten years from now?" "What do you need to do before tip-off?"

After every question, he gave them a few moments to write and reflect. If you watch Buzz's sideline demeanor, you could draw the conclusion that he's more emotional than cerebral. I haven't met many people who are more mindful than he is.

After that meditation, Buzz complimented his players on how they had handled their day off. Then he reminded them of their team theme: #getbetter. Take that, Toyota! Then Buzz did one last thing. I'm guessing the players already knew how many games they had played, including wins and losses. Buzz reminded them of how many practices they'd had—seventy-four. The Hokies' Sweet Sixteen matchup with Duke wasn't a one-off. It was a cumulative effort. They wound the clock seventy-four times.

How do we wind the clock? By getting better every day! At what? At everything!

Considered by many to be the greatest cellist to ever draw the bow, Pablo Casals's career spanned many decades. He played a private concert for Queen Victoria when he was twenty-two. He played for President Kennedy when he was eighty-six. Casals lived to the age of ninety-six, and in his eighties, he was still practicing four or five hours a day. When asked why, he said, "Because I think I am making progress."[18]

KINGFISHER

If I believe in anything, I believe in a long obedience in the same direction. It was Eugene Peterson who wrote a book by that title, and his life exemplified it.[19] Not long before he died, I was part of a small group that gathered to honor his life and legacy. Eugene shared a few life lessons that I will long remember. But even more than his words, I remember the twinkle in his eye. Time had taken its toll, like it does on all of us, but he was still standing, still smiling.

How did Eugene wind the clock? The secret lies in a story he shared about the kingfisher, a bird famous for its fishing finesse. Eugene was sitting on the deck of his Montana lake house one day, watching a kingfisher try to catch its prey. He counted the number of attempts. "It took thirty-seven tries to catch a fish," said Eugene, "and he's the kingfisher!" After a dramatic pause, Eugene asked a pointed question: "How many times have you tried?"

It was Eugene's inimitable way of reminding us that we give up too quickly, too easily! That's the lesson eighty-five years of living had taught him, and it's a lesson better learned sooner than later. There is a kind of power that is often overlooked and underappreciated—*staying power*! Especially in our quick-fix culture! Staying power is refusing to quit, come hell or high water. It will not be denied.

Discerning God's timing is not easy. Trusting His timing is even harder. Please know this: God is counting. He counts our tears. He counts our random acts of kindness. He counts our steps of faith. He even counts the hairs on our heads. God is really good at keeping track of what we do right and rewarding us for it. Do not grow weary in well doing![20]

If the kingfisher had given up after the thirty-sixth attempt, it would have given up one attempt too soon. Like the kingfisher, I don't think we should be embarrassed at all by the number of tries it takes to catch a fish! If anything, we ought to be proud of the fact that we didn't give up!

God hasn't given up on you.

Don't give up on God.

Wind the clock with faith, hope, and love!

Habit 7—Seed the Clouds

Sow today what you want to see tomorrow.

On November 13, 1946, a plane took off from the Schenectady County Airport with a rather unique payload—six pounds of dry ice. Its mission? To seed the clouds with solidified carbon dioxide, in hopes of creating enough condensation to cause precipitation.

For many months prior to that flight, a chemist named Vincent Schaefer had been conducting clandestine experiments at General Electric Research Laboratory, the House of Magic. Using a GE freezer chilled to subzero temperatures, Schaefer created clouds using his breath and seeded them with different chemical substances. After many failed attempts, on a hot July day, Schaefer added some dry ice to his freezer. That dry ice caused a chemical reaction and catalyzed snow crystals. A few months later, it was time for a field test.

Upon takeoff, Schaefer flew his single-propeller plane into a cumulus cloud and dumped the dry ice. Eyewitnesses on the ground said that the cloud seemed to explode. The subsequent snowfall was visible for forty miles. The *GE Monogram* had a little fun with Schaefer's breakthrough: "Schaefer made it snow this afternoon over Pittsfield! Next week he walks on water."[1]

The science of seeding clouds may be a modern-day marvel, but the idea is as old as the prophet Elijah. After a famine that lasted three and a half years, Elijah seeded the clouds with a brave prayer.

> Elijah climbed to the top of Mount Carmel and bowed low to the ground and prayed with his face between his knees.[2]

There are lots of ways to seed the clouds. Humility catalyzes God's favor. Generosity activates reciprocity, which I detail in my book *Double Blessing*. And old-fashioned obedience sets the table for unborn tomorrows. You can seed the clouds in many different ways, but none are more powerful than prayer!

When was the last time you found yourself doubled over in prayer? The posture that Elijah assumes indicates profound humility and extreme intensity. He's not just praying; he's believing in God for a miracle. I have no issue with short blessings before meals. Why? I believe in eating food while it's hot. That said, there are moments when you need to press in and pray through. You need to seed the clouds with contending prayer.

In our quest to win the day, we have buried dead yesterdays and imagined unborn tomorrows. We've explored six habits—*flip the script, kiss the wave, eat the frog, fly the kite, cut the rope,* and *wind the clock.* There is one more habit we must put into practice if we want to stress less and accomplish more. You have to *seed the clouds.* How? By taking proactive measures today that will produce desired outcomes tomorrow. Simply put, sow today what you want to see tomorrow! Identify the daily rituals that have the highest return on investment and the daily habits that are high leverage points, and then prioritize them. Right at the top of the list? Don't underestimate the power of a single brave prayer! Of course, that's the tip of the iceberg.

The only ceiling on your intimacy with God and your impact on the world is daily spiritual disciplines. For me, winning the day starts with my daily Bible reading plan—that is the seedbed of faith. And I don't just read through it; I meditate on it. Meditation is more than daydreaming; it's cloud seeding! Reading gets us into God's Word. Meditation gets God's Word into us. Let me bring this seventh habit down to earth.

You can seed the clouds with something as simple as a smile. You can shift the atmosphere with your attitude. You can alter the trajectory of someone's life with a small act of kindness. You seed the clouds with every sacrifice you make, every risk you take.

In 1987, Howard Schultz faced a defining decision. He was offered the option of purchasing a small chain of coffee shops with a strange name, Starbucks. To buy or not to buy? That was the question. It seems like a no-brainer now, but it was a bold move back then. Schultz likened the $4 million price tag to a salmon attempting to swallow a whale! That's eating the frog, next level.

> *This is my moment,* I thought. *If I don't seize the opportunity, if I don't step out of my comfort zone and risk it all, if I let too much time tick on, my moment will pass.* I knew that if I didn't take advantage of this opportunity, I would replay it in my mind for my whole life, wondering: *What if?*[3]

Howard Schultz rolled the dice, taking an enormous risk to pursue his passion for all things coffee. Starbucks stock went public five years later, on June 26, 1992. It was the second most actively traded stock on the NASDAQ that day. By closing bell, its market capitalization was $273 million,[4] making Howard Schultz a multimillionaire.

Howard Schultz is a rainmaker, but make no mistake, he didn't get lucky. He seeded the clouds with a calculated risk. It was vision that catalyzed that chain reaction. Hindsight is twenty-twenty. If we all knew then what we all know now, there would be many more multimillionaires. Right? We would have invested in Starbucks the day we started drinking caramel macchiatos.

In his book *On Paradise Drive,* David Brooks offers an interesting analysis of the American psyche. We are a future-minded people, and this type of mindset Brooks calls the Paradise Spell. It's "the capacity to see the *present* from the vantage point of the *future*."[5] There is a down-side to this future-mindedness, and it's our inability to be present in the present. That said, it's also an expression of faith. "It starts with imagination—the ability to see a vision with detail and vividness, as if it already existed. Then the future-minded person is able to think backward."[6]

That is precisely the way God works in our lives! He begins with the end in mind, providentially preparing good works in advance. Then God works backward. Seeding the clouds is exercising our faith by identifying God-honoring, God-sized goals, then reverse engineering them into daily habits.

Seeding clouds is dreaming big by thinking long, and it starts with praying hard. Praying without planning is a waste of time, while plan-ning without praying is a waste of energy. It's also called the sin of pre-sumption. The good news? The more you pray, the bigger you dream. And the bigger you dream, the more you have to pray!

Let me double back to Elijah one more time. At first, there was no visible evidence of God answering his prayer for rain. That is when most of us give up, but Elijah doubled down.

> "Go and look toward the sea," he told his servant. And he went
>   up and looked.
> "There is nothing there," he said.
> Seven times Elijah said, "Go back."
> The seventh time the servant reported, "A cloud as small as a
>   man's hand is rising from the sea."[7]

The greatest tragedy in life is that prayers go unanswered because they go unasked. God won't answer 100 percent of the prayers you don't pray! While we're on the subject, you won't accomplish 100 percent of the goals you don't set. But let me flip that script. Prayer is the way we write history before it happens! It's the difference between letting things happen and making things happen. You've got to pray through to the breakthrough! If you want to win the day, you can't wish upon a star. You have to seed the clouds with brave prayers!

In the first century BC, the nation of Israel was devastated by a severe famine. An entire generation of Jewish people was in jeopardy. That's when an ancient sage named Honi took his staff and drew a circle in the sand. He knelt in that circle and prayed this prayer:

> By Your great Name I swear that I will not move from here until You have mercy on Your children.[8]

Honi was criticized for his holy audacity, but it's hard to argue with a miracle. As that prayer went up, rain came down. Honi earned his nickname: the Circle Maker. It's the prayer that saved a generation, the generation before Jesus.

Don't underestimate the power of a single seed, a single prayer! It has the power to change anything, change everything. The same goes for the seeds of faith, hope, and love. Don't worry about the outcomes; focus on inputs. We plant and water, but God gives the increase!

Let me ask a simple question: If you plant carrot seeds, what do you get? The easy answer is carrots. How about pumpkin seeds? The obvious answer is pumpkins. What if you don't plant anything? You might think the answer is *nothing,* but you'll actually get weeds. The simple truth is this: You cannot break the law of sowing and reaping. It will make or break you!

Do you know the first thing Noah did after getting a vision to build a very big boat? According to rabbinic tradition, he planted trees! Why? He knew he'd need lots of planks! That's how every vision begins. Go ahead and dream big, but you have to start small.

In 1979, Jadav Payeng started planting trees on the island of Majuli.[9] Why? Monsoons were flooding the Brahmaputra River and eroding the island at an alarming rate. Majuli had lost half of its land mass in the previous one hundred years. Jadav started seeding the clouds by literally seeding the earth. Four decades later, his forest is larger than Central Park in New York City. His reforestation efforts have not only slowed the erosion but also repopulated species of animals that had almost gone extinct. There's even a herd of elephants living on the island.[10]

Don't despise the day of small beginnings or clouds the size of a man's hand. God can move mountains with a mustard seed of faith! What is your God-sized vision? What is your God-given passion? What are you waiting for?

Seed the clouds!

13

Now or Never

There is no time like the present.

On May 29, 1832, a twenty-year-old French mathematician sat down and wrote a sixty-page mathematical masterpiece in one sitting. "[This paper], if judged by the novelty and profundity of ideas it contains," said Hermann Weyl, "is perhaps the most substantial piece of writing in the whole literature of mankind."[1]

While still a teenager, Évariste Galois determined "a necessary and sufficient condition for a polynomial to be solvable by radicals."[2] I must have missed that math class, because I have no earthly idea what that even means! But in doing so, Galois had solved a 350-year-old mathematical mystery.

Évariste Galois was a wunderkind, no doubt. He laid the foundation for a branch of algebra known as group theory—a building block for computer science, coding theory, and cryptography. Two hundred years later, a Galois connection is "a way of solving challenging mathematical problems by translating them into different mathematical domains."[3] Again, Galois had just turned twenty!

According to E. T. Bell, the paper Galois wrote on May 29 "will keep generations of mathematicians busy for hundreds of years."[4] This raises the question: How did Évariste Galois synthesize so many abstract ideas in a single day? The answer? Évariste Galois lived May 29, 1832, like it was the last day of his life. Why? Because he was quite certain it would be! Challenged to a duel by his rival, Perscheux d'Herbinville, Galois knew it was *now or never*! The duel doubled as a deadline, and it's amazing what a deadline will do. It fired his synapses and focused his mind. In the margins of that masterpiece, Galois repeatedly scribbled, "I have not time; I have not time."[5]

Seeding the clouds is *not* an unsanctified sense of urgency. That's called stress! It's not trying to keep up with the Kardashians. It's not even trying to get ahead. Seeding the clouds is the sacred awareness that you've got one shot at this thing called life. All you've got is this moment—right here, right now.

Decision Fatigue

I have a word to the wise. If you ever find yourself before a parole board, try to secure the earliest time slot available. Why? The disposition of the judge who presides over your case may have less bearing on the ruling than the time of day it's scheduled. My grandfather was a judge, so I say that with all due respect.

In a study conducted by the National Academy of Sciences, 1,112 rulings by an Israeli parole board were examined over a ten-month period. Seventy percent of prisoners whose cases were reviewed early in the morning were granted parole. The probability of a favorable ruling declined, then returned to early-morning levels each time the judges took a break to eat. Prisoners who appeared late in the day, however, were granted parole only 10 percent of the time. No, they didn't save the worst for last. The authors of that study cited decision fatigue as the primary reason for the declining percentage of successful parole appeals.[6]

Decision fatigue is the deterioration of our ability to make good decisions after making lots of decisions. Decision-making takes mental energy. Like with physical exercise, we fatigue over time. We lose motivation. We lose focus. We lose willpower. No one knows this better than parents of toddlers! You want to limit your children's screen time—

I know you do. But by the end of the day, you just need to stop the insanity!

On the night before Jesus's crucifixion, His disciples made some bad decisions. Peter reacted rashly, cutting off the right ear of the high priest's servant.[7] Then he denied Jesus three times.[8] One of His other disciples even ran off naked.[9] It got pretty ugly pretty quickly. But do you remember the context? More specifically, the time of day?

Piecing together the timeline, we can determine that it was right around midnight. I'm not letting the disciples off the hook, but they were dog tired. In fact, they had already fallen asleep twice![10] Part of what contributed to their poor decisions was good old-fashioned fatigue. Disciples aren't exempt. Judges aren't exempt. And neither are we. "I don't think this is at all unique to judges," said Jonathan Levav, one of the researchers involved in the study. "I think you would find the same thing with doctors or with admissions officers or with funding decisions."[11]

The ramifications of decision fatigue are felt in dozens of ways in every arena of life. According to one estimate, we make approximately thirty-five thousand decisions every day.[12] One key to making good decisions is making fewer decisions, and that's where predecisions come into play. That said, seeding the clouds is not one and done. You have to hit reset throughout the day.

SELAH

There is a curious word that surfaces in the Psalms seventy-one times. Its etymological origins are a mystery, but it appears to be an ancient musical notation. The word *selah* represents a rest. If the Sabbath is a whole rest, selah is an eighth rest. It's little moments during the day when you aren't conscious of the clock.

Beethoven's Symphony no. 5 in C Minor has an iconic opening. But I don't want to talk about the four-note opening you can hear in your head: *Da, da, da, dum.* The symphony actually begins with an eighth rest before the famous four notes! That rest is a sonic buffer to help the audience switch gears. We need a few more eighth rests, don't we? Selah helps us be fully present. It also turns up the volume on the still, small voice of the Holy Spirit.

The English poet John Donne said, "I neglect God and his angels, for the noise of a fly."[13] All too often, the fly in our phone! There are many more distractions now than there were then. How do we stay focused? Stay positive? Stay centered?

One, *start your day with silence.*

I know this is easier said than done, even when we're all alone. You can turn your phone to Do Not Disturb, which I highly recommend. Unfortunately, the voices in our heads don't have that setting. Silence takes deliberate practice. Of course, noise-canceling headphones help too! If you really want to wind the clock and seed the clouds, try turning your phone off on your day off!

The seventeenth-century French philosopher Blaise Pascal said, "The sole cause of man's unhappiness is that he does not know how to stay quietly in his room."[14] That's quite a statement, but it's not an overstatement. God speaks loudest when we're quietest. We all need a little peace and quiet now and then. That's the eighth rest the psalmist called selah.

Two, *take your thoughts captive.*

One way you seed the clouds is by focusing your mind on things that are good and right and pure and just.[15] Your focus will determine your reality! Selah is stopping long enough to smell the roses. Or as Jesus put it, "Consider the lilies."[16] Something as simple as a gratitude journal can totally alter your reality by shifting your focus! And it's not just the top-of-the-Empire-State-Building moments that you should focus on. When you look for little things to be grateful for, it has a way of turning minutes into moments.

Remember Henry David Thoreau? He cut the rope and made the move to Walden Pond. While he was there, he seeded the clouds with a daily regimen. He took long walks in the afternoon, equipped with an array of primitive tools—"his hat for specimen-collecting, a heavy book to press plants, a spyglass to watch birds, his walking stick to take measurements, and small scraps of paper for jotting down notes."[17] At Ralph Waldo Emerson's urging, Thoreau had been journaling since graduating from Harvard in 1837. But he took journaling to the next level while at Walden. Thoreau's real masterpiece isn't *Walden*. It's the two-million-word journal where he recorded his daily observations. Every day, Thoreau filled page after page with "a stream-of-consciousness flow of words." One of his biographers, Laura Dassow Walls, noted, "From this point, Thoreau did not stop doing this, ever—not until, dying and almost too weak to hold a pen, he crafted one final entry."[18]

Three, *play the long game.*

Seeding the clouds is leaving a legacy on earth while laying up treasures in heaven. It's not just playing the long game; it's playing the infinite game. Only one life will soon be past; only what's done for Christ will last. "Our imagination so magnifies the present because we are continually thinking about it," said Blaise Pascal, "and so reduces eternity, because we do not think about it, that we turn eternity into nothing and nothing into eternity."[19] In a world where everything seems to happen in real time, we need a reality check. We've got to dream bigger than fifteen minutes of fame. We've got to think longer than news cycles. Seeding the clouds is planting what someone else will harvest. Why? Because someone did the same for you!

ENJOY THE JOURNEY

In the first sermon I ever preached at National Community Church, I cited a sociological study involving fifty people over the age of ninety-five. Collectively, they had more than five thousand years of life experience. The survey consisted of one question: *If you had your life to live all over again, what would you do differently?* Three replies emerged as a consensus. One, *risk more.* Two, *reflect more.* Three, *do more things that live on after you die.*

I'd second all three of those notions, but let me add one more to the mix. *Enjoy the journey!* Life is too short not to enjoy every age, every stage. I believe the best is yet to come, but the grass is *not* greener on the other side!

If you don't enjoy life *now,* you won't enjoy it *then.*

If you don't enjoy life *here,* you won't enjoy it *there.*

Don't fall into the when/then trap. What is it? It's thinking we'll be happy when we find ourselves in a certain set of circumstances. *When I graduate or when I get married or when I get my dream job, then I'll be happy.* No you won't. *When I have kids or get the promotion or get out of debt, then I'll be happy.* Trust me—it never ends! *When our kids are out of diapers or we reach retirement or we're financially independent, then life will be good.* Quit lying to yourself. Let's call it what it is—someday sickness.

We have to guard the present against two threats, two thieves. The first is past-tense guilt. The second is future-tense anxiety. They come to kill, steal, and destroy. How do we guard against them? We make a pre-decision to enjoy the journey—no matter what, no matter when, no matter where!

Seeding the clouds is *not* wishing on a star. It doesn't wait for perfect conditions. Remember habit 3, *eat the frog*? You don't *find* time; you *make* time. In the same vein, you don't *find* opportunity. You *make* opportunity.

> Whoever watches the wind will not plant;
>> whoever looks at the clouds will not reap.[20]

That verse of Scripture proved to be the cure for both my perfectionism and my procrastination. If you wait for perfect conditions, you'll be waiting till the Lord returns. If you wait until you're ready, you'll be waiting the rest of your life. You'll never find perfect conditions, and you'll never be ready. My mantra? If you get a green light from God—go, set, ready!

The writer of Ecclesiastes said: "Sow your seed in the morning, and at evening let your hands not be idle."[21] Solomon doesn't specify whether we should seed the ground or seed the clouds, but it's the same difference. You've got to sow the seed of faith, the seed of love, the seed of obedience.

Andy Stanley once said, "You are probably never going to be more than about 80 percent certain."[22] That single sentence changed my life and leadership. If you're looking to get married, I'd aim a little higher than 80 percent certainty. But I've applied this 80 percent rule to just about everything I do, and it has helped me overcome my perfectionism and my procrastination. Don't just look at the clouds and daydream, fly a plane of dry ice into them!

POUND THE PAVEMENT

On September 26, 1855, a sixteen-year-old John D. Rockefeller walked into a Cleveland merchant company, Hewitt and Tuttle, and got a job as an assistant bookkeeper. It was his first job. He made fifty cents a day, and he loved every minute of it. For the rest of his life, Rockefeller observed September 26 as a personal holiday. He called it Job Day, and he considered it more significant than his birthday. "All my future seemed to hinge on that day," he reminisced.[23]

Rockefeller had two great ambitions: the first was to make $100,000, and the second was to live to one hundred.[24] He fell short of his second goal, dying at the age of ninety-seven. He may have aimed a little low on the first goal. Rockefeller's net worth when he died, adjusted for inflation, was $340 billion.[25] Not bad for someone who started out making fifty cents a day!

Rockefeller ranks as the wealthiest American of all time, and his philanthropy set the standard at the turn of the twentieth century. Beginning with his first paycheck, he tithed 10 percent of all his earnings to his church, and he gave more than $500 million to scientific and educational undertakings through the Rockefeller Foundation. I consider myself one of his beneficiaries, having attended the school he founded and funded, the University of Chicago. My dorm was right across the

street from Rockefeller Memorial Chapel and its seventy-two-bell caril-
lon, but I digress.

In August 1855, Rockefeller left his boardinghouse at eight o'clock
every morning and went door to door, trying to land a job until the
close of business. He came up empty, but he kept at it. He did this six
days a week for six straight weeks. For those keeping score at home,
that's a thirty-six-day losing streak. Most of us would have gotten discouraged, but Rockefeller grew more determined. When you finally
land a job after thirty-six days of pounding the pavement, you are less
likely to take that job for granted. In fact, you celebrate the day you got
it as a personal holiday the rest of your life!

"One is tempted to say that his real life began on that day," wrote one
of Rockefeller's biographers, "that he was born again in business as he
would be in the Erie Street Baptist Mission Church."[26]

Seeding the clouds isn't waiting to win the lottery! It's pounding the
pavement. It's not letting things happen; it's making things happen.
Don't try to manufacture the miracle and get ahead of God. But don't sit
around twiddling your thumbs either. We need a holy urgency. Not the
kind that is born of nervousness; the kind that is born of God-given
passion. The kind that comes from a place of rest, an eighth rest.

PERSONAL HOLIDAYS

There are defining days that mark our lives forever, like Rockefeller's
Job Day. Like Rockefeller, we must turn them into memorial days.
How? That's up to you.

> One person considers one day more sacred than another; an-
> other considers every day alike. Each of them should be fully
> convinced in their own mind.[27]

It almost seems like doublespeak, but this exhortation is worth a
double take. In one sense, winning the day is treating every day like it's

the first day and last day of your life. In that sense, every day is sacred. That said, some days are more sacred than others. I know that sounds contradictory, but truth is a two-sided coin that requires flipping.

Every day should be stewarded as sacred—heads.

Some days tip the sacred scale more than others—tails.

For better or for worse, there are days that define us. They alter the reality of our lives ever after. They introduce a new chapter, a new normal. Some moments are as wonderful as walking down the aisle on your wedding day or walking out of the hospital with a new baby. Other moments are as painful as being served divorce papers, getting a difficult diagnosis, or learning about the death of a loved one. One way or the other, those are the moments that mark us. And we must mark them.

What are your memorial days?

What days do you celebrate as personal holidays?

You don't have to dot the calendar with lots of days. In fact, the fewer and further between, the more meaningful they will be. Rockefeller made billions of dollars, but it was a fifty-cent payday that kept him grounded, kept him grateful. It not only helped Rockefeller win the day, but it also helped him win the years as part of his annual rhythm.

I've already shared one of my memorial days, July 2, 2016. That is the day God healed my asthma. I not only celebrate it annually; I actually keep track of the days I've been inhaler-free. Let me share one more personal holiday in hopes of helping you identify yours.

July 23, 2000, came very close to being the last day of my life! That is the day my intestines ruptured and I was rushed into emergency surgery at two o'clock in the morning. I spent two days on a respirator, fighting for my life. I lost twenty-five pounds in one week, along with a foot of intestines. The scar all the way down the middle of my abdomen is a constant reminder of the worst day of my life, the hardest year of my life. I wouldn't want to go through anything like that again, but I wouldn't trade it for anything in the world either. I now consider it one of the best days of my life. Why? You don't take a single day for granted after that. Every single day is seen for what it is—a gift from God. I don't get a cake, but I do celebrate July 23 as my "second birthday." I commemorate it the way Rockefeller commemorated Job Day.

If you're anything like me, there are some days you don't want to remember. The memory of them triggers painful emotions. I'm certainly not suggesting that you celebrate them, but you must commemorate them. If you don't define them, they will define you.

The day Joseph's brothers sold him into slavery was the low point of his life. It was also the turning point. It took thirteen years to flip that script, but Joseph kept seeding the clouds. Some days, that involved resisting temptation. Other days, it involved interpreting dreams. Either way, Joseph learned to leverage each day for God's glory.

Observe This Day

When God set Israel up as a new nation, He did quite a bit of calendaring. He established a rhythm of work and rest, a six-to-one ratio. He established days of fasting and days of feasting. Three major holidays dot the Jewish calendar, and each one was commemorated with tremendous specificity and intentionality. The Passover was celebrated with a well-choreographed meal, making it a little like our Thanksgiving Day. Of course, its closest equivalent may be the Fourth of July since the Israelites were celebrating their freedom.

> On this very day have I brought your hosts out of the land of Egypt; therefore shall you observe this day throughout your generations as an ordinance forever.
>
> In the first month, on the fourteenth day of the month at evening, you shall eat unleavened bread [and continue] until the twenty-first day of the month at evening.[28]

The second pilgrimage feast, Pentecost, was like a ticker-tape parade. And the Feast of Tabernacles must have felt a little like the Burning Man festival because it involved camping out for a week.

Along with the three pilgrimage feasts, the Jewish people celebrated the first day of every month, Rosh Chodesh. They began the new year, Rosh Hashanah, with Ten Days of Repentance. There were minor fasting days, like the Tenth of Tevet.[29] There were High Holy Days like Yom Kippur. And after the Passover, they counted the forty-nine days—the sephirah days—leading up to Pentecost, when they would commemorate the giving of the Torah. The Hebrew word *sephirah* literally means "counting." The bottom line? There was a rhyme and reason to every season!

We tend to glaze over when it comes to names and places and dates. We have flashbacks to pop quizzes in history class. So we bypass the begats and detour around the dates. I get it—they feel like random facts and figures. But the Jewish calendar makes a beautiful melody. In fact, the Israelites initiated those celebrations with music.[30] We may not celebrate the same holidays the same way, but we've got to find our own harmony between chronos and kairos.

When it comes to personal holidays, to each his own. Find a way to make them meaningful. If you don't, the days seem long and the years seem short. On the day I release a new book, our family celebrates with a special dinner. Why? Every book deserves a birthday party! Release day is the day we tie off the umbilical cord—it's out of my hands and in God's hands. Every book takes on a life of its own as we launch it into the world.

Is there a day that tips the sacred scale? Turn it into a holiday! While you're at it, celebrate each day for what it is—a once-in-a-lifetime, never-to-be-repeated miracle. If you want to win the day, you've got to live that way! You seed the clouds by celebrating what you want to see more of.

DAY BY DAY

In the movie *Meet the Parents,* the character played by Ben Stiller stumbles and bumbles his way through an awkward predinner prayer. But it finishes with quite a flourish: "Three things we pray: to love Thee more dearly, to see Thee more clearly, to follow Thee more nearly." Then he adds a little punch line to his prayer: "day by day by day."[31] I laughed out loud the first time I heard it. What's even funnier is the fact that it's a *real* prayer. After seeing the movie, I came across the original prayer in a book on Ignatian spirituality. It dates all the way back to the thirteenth century and Richard of Chichester, a bishop and chancellor of Oxford. The only difference between the two prayers is that Stiller added an extra day to Richard's "day by day." I like Stiller's version even better!

"Day by day" is a mantra repeated throughout Scripture.

The pillar of cloud led them forward *day by day*.[32]

Your strength shall be renewed *day by day* like morning dew.[33]

Outwardly we are wasting away, yet inwardly we are being renewed *day by day*.[34]

Give us *day by day* our daily bread.[35]

If you want to stress less and accomplish more, you've got to live day by day. That brings us all the way back to William Osler's exhortation to live in day-tight compartments. Remember the seven-word question? Let me ask it one more time:

Can you do it for a day?

It's time to put this into deliberate practice. Don't be overwhelmed by the number of problems you need to solve, the number of changes you want to make, or the number of goals you're going after. Number your days! How? One at a time. Don't worry about next week, next month, or next year. All you have to do is seed the clouds, and God will make it rain. Go 1–0 today and tomorrow will be better than today.

Remember my original hypothesis? *Almost anybody can accomplish almost anything if they work at it long enough, hard enough, and smart enough.* I hope you believe it more now than you did at the beginning of this book. No habit is too hard, with God's help. No goal is too big, if it glorifies God. Why not you? Why not now?

There is no time like the present.

Seed the clouds!

Epilogue

The Game with Minutes

Live like there's no tomorrow.

On May 25, 1979, Denis Waitley was desperately trying to catch a flight from Chicago to Los Angeles for a speaking engagement. There are easier airports to run through than O'Hare! When he arrived at his gate, they had just closed the Jetway. Denis begged them to let him on that airplane. No luck! Out of breath and out of patience, he made his way to the ticket counter to register a complaint and rebook his travel. While he was waiting in line, an announcement came over the airport intercom. AA Flight 191 to Los Angeles had crashed upon takeoff.

The engine on the left wing of that McDonnell Douglas DC-10 separated from the airplane right after takeoff. The unbalanced aerodynamics caused the plane to roll, a roll from which it could not recover. All 258 passengers, as well as thirteen crew members, died in the crash. It was the deadliest aviation accident in United States history.

That near-death experience had a life-altering impact on Denis Waitley. Had he been on time, it would have been the last day of his life. Needless to say, he never registered his complaint. In fact, he never returned his ticket for Flight 191. He took his paper ticket and put it in a visible place in his office.

On difficult days, the days when Denis Waitley felt like throwing in the towel, all it took was one glance at that ticket to regain perspective.

That ticket was a constant reminder that every day is a gift. It helped him live his life in day-tight compartments. Denis Waitley's ticket for Flight 191 is what I would call a life symbol—a symbol from the past that gives meaning to the present and functions as a compass for the future.

For John D. Rockefeller, it was his first paycheck.

For Elisha Otis, it was an ax.

For John Wooden, it was a pair of socks.

For Elon Musk, it was a Commodore VIC-20 computer.

For Homan Walsh, it was a kite.

What are the symbols from your past, painful and joyful, that make each day more meaningful? My life symbols include an oxygen mask from one of my asthma-related hospitalizations; the graduate assessment that showed a low aptitude for writing; a brick from the crack house that is now Ebenezers Coffeehouse; and my grandfather's well-worn, well-read, well-lived Bible that is almost a century old.

In one sense, those life symbols are worthless. Anybody want an old oxygen mask? I didn't think so! But to me, they're priceless! Why? They represent top-of-the-Empire-State-Building and bottom-of-the-Grand-Canyon moments. They taught me lessons I can't afford to forget. They represent minutes that turned into moments that I will remember forever.

What does any of that have to do with winning the day? Trust me—this is more than a walk down memory lane. Life symbols are the key to getting where God wants us to go. They're the key to becoming who God wants us to be. They're the key to unleashing the power of twenty-four hours. Life symbols help us flip the script, kiss the wave, eat the frog, fly the kite, cut the rope, wind the clock, and seed the clouds!

LIFE SYMBOLS

Remember David versus Goliath? After defeating Goliath, David took Goliath's armor and parked it in his tent.[1] We read right past this detail, but it's a big deal. And I mean that literally. Goliath's armor weighed 125 pounds. I'm not sure David weighed much more than that. Why would he go to all the trouble of undressing Goliath and putting his armor in his tent? If Saul's armor didn't fit him, Goliath's armor would have fit him even worse! If you can't wear it, why save it?

Like Denis Waitley's ticket to Flight 191, Goliath's armor functioned as a life symbol. When David got discouraged, one glance at Goliath's armor reminded him that he was nobody's underdog. That armor fueled holy confidence for the rest of his life. I bet David marked his calendar, celebrating it as Giant Day ever after. Putting Goliath's armor in his tent was a stroke of genius. We might want to follow suit—pun intended.

According to developmental psychologists, if an object is removed from a baby's field of view, it's as if that object ceases to exist. That's why peekaboo is so much fun with young children! They have not developed the understanding of object permanence. Simply put, *out of sight, out of mind*. We never really outgrow this tendency, do we? This is why we build memorials and celebrate holidays.

We have a tendency to remember what we should forget and forget what we should remember. The way we overcome spiritual amnesia is by building altars. What do we put on them? Life symbols. Those life symbols don't just point back to the past; they point to the future. Our future-tense faith is a function of God's past-tense faithfulness. The older we get, the more faith we should have! Why? More testimonies.

There is a branch of philosophy called teleology. It's the doctrine of design, and it's the way we connect the dots just like David did with the bears and the lions. For us, the arrow of time points from the past toward the future. God is working the opposite way! Not only are His eternal plans and purposes counterintuitive; they are also counterclockwise. God has already prepared good works for us in advance.[2] They seem future tense to us, but they are past tense to God. Remember the walls of Jericho? Even before they came crashing down, God declared it done![3]

That brings us all the way back to where we began—the eternal now.

Even when we can't see it, heaven is invading earth. Even when we don't feel it, eternity is invading time every second of every minute of every hour of every day!

Quit wasting guilt on yesterday.

Quit wasting worry on tomorrow.

It's time to start living in day-tight compartments.

Redeem the Time

"Make some new experiments."[4] That is the timeless challenge issued by Thomas Shepard, a Puritan pastor and key figure in establishing Harvard College. Shepard believed in approaching our spiritual lives like a scientific experiment, and I couldn't agree more. "Make a new experiment on secret prayer," he said. "And then come forth from your secret prayer and make immediate experiment on more love, and more patience, and more consideration for other men."[5]

Now there's an idea!

What if we approached every day that way?

Don't just fly the kite; turn it into a lightning rod like Benjamin Franklin.

Don't just eat the frog; dissect it like Theodore Graves Hulett.

Don't just wind the clock; redeem the time like Frank Laubach.

On January 30, 1930, Frank Laubach initiated an experiment he called "the game with minutes." He referred to it as "a new game for something as old as Enoch."[6] The goal? Continual awareness of God's presence. Laubach turned his everyday life into a laboratory and started experimenting with his spirituality. Six months into his research, he wrote these words in his prayer journal:

> Last Monday was the most completely successful day of my life to date, so far as giving my day in complete and continuous surrender to God is concerned. . . . As I looked at people with a

love God gave, they looked back and acted as though they wanted to go with me. I felt then that for a day I saw a little of that marvelous pull that Jesus had as He walked along the road day after day "God-intoxicated" and radiant with the endless communion of His soul with God.[7]

The greatest challenge to this kind of communion with God? Laubach isolated our root problem: "We shall not become like Christ," he said, "until we give Him more time."[8] Remember, you won't *find* time. You have to *make* time. How much time? Laubach started with one second of every minute. You cannot win the day until you win the hour, and you cannot win the hour until you win the minute. Don't despise the day of small beginnings—or the hour or the minute!

"You will find this just as easy," said Laubach, "and just as hard as forming any other habit."[9] It takes deliberate practice to seed the clouds! That goes for flipping the script, kissing the wave, eating the frog, flying the kite, cutting the rope, and winding the clock too!

But over time, you'll win more days than you lose. And the compound interest will catch up with you. "The results . . . begin to show clearly in a month," said Laubach. "They grow rich after six months, and glorious after ten years."[10]

We overestimate what we can accomplish in the short term, but we underestimate what God can accomplish with long obedience in the same direction. If you play the long game, your life will outlast you. It's called legacy, and it's the cumulative effect of a life well lived. What is a life well lived? It's winning the day—day by day by day.

I've already appraised the value of a single day. In God's economy, a day is like a thousand years. God takes every day seriously, and so should we. How? By stewarding every day as a gift from Him. That said, I want us to end on a more playful note. Winning the day is *fun*. Think of it as *the game with minutes*. The goal of the game? Unleashing the power of twenty-four hours!

ANOTHER DAY, ANOTHER ADVENTURE

Many years ago, I spent a life-changing week in the Galápagos Islands. That archipelago may be the closest thing to the Garden of Eden left on earth. We saw pelicans that looked like prehistoric pterodactyls dive-bomb into the ocean and come up with breakfast in their beaks. We came face to face with giant tortoises and marine iguanas. We went swimming with sea lions, which is more dangerous than I realized at the time. Oh, we also went cliff jumping at Las Grietas. My legs were black and blue for a month, but the adrenaline rush was worth it.

At one point during that unforgettable week, I found a Spanish Sprite can. *Yo hablo un poco español,* but I knew enough to translate what it said. In fact, these four words have been a life motto ever since: *Otra Día, Otra Aventura.*

Another day, another adventure.

Not every day is as amazing as the extraordinary days I spent in the Galápagos, but even the most mundane of days is no less miraculous! Remember, you're on a planet that is spinning at one thousand miles per hour and speeding through space at sixty-six thousand miles per hour. We do a celestial 360 every twenty-four hours! That's worth celebrating every day, isn't it?

"This is the *day* that the Lord has made; let us rejoice and be glad in it."[11]

"Give us this *day* our daily bread."[12]

"His mercies . . . are new *every morning*."[13]

"Surely goodness and mercy shall follow me *all the days of my life*."[14]

You can accomplish almost anything if you work at it long enough, hard enough, and smart enough. It's time to unleash the power of twenty-four hours! You've got this. Why? God's got this! It's time to stress less and accomplish more.

Go win the day!

Acknowledgments

It takes a team to accomplish a dream, and that's certainly true of *Win the Day*. I owe a debt of gratitude to WaterBrook Multnomah for publishing my first book, *In a Pit with a Lion on a Snowy Day*. I'm grateful for the continued friendship and partnership.

Thanks to Tina, Laura, Campbell, and Andrew for your faith in this project, as evidenced by your consistent encouragement. I'm grateful for the way you rally around your authors!

Andrew, you have wisdom beyond your years, and your editing is second to none! I also need to give credit where credit is due: the cover is all you!

Chris, thanks for investing your heart and soul in this book. The same goes for you, Brett and Beverly and Leslie and Ginia. Grateful for the way you open doors to get this message out.

Thanks to Mark and Kris and Joe for the way you turn words into fonts and images into covers!

Thanks to Helen for your patience with my perfectionism! Thanks to Kayla, Kathy, and Rachel, as well as Julia, Angela, Virginia, and Ruby for your eye for detail.

Thanks to Kim and Julie for putting your fingerprints on this project.

Thanks to the entire sales team—Lori, William, Steve, Katie, Todd, Andrew, and Ashley. Without you, this book doesn't get into people's hands and hearts!

I want to thank my agent, Esther Fedorkevich, and the entire

Fedd Agency team. I know you don't just represent my books; you read them and live them!

Finally, thanks to my family. Lora, your wisdom is woven into this book! And thanks to my church family. I'm eternally grateful for the privilege of pastoring National Community Church. My prayer is that NCC is always the primary beneficiary of my books.

Notes

INTRODUCTION: DAY-TIGHT COMPARTMENTS

1. *The Principles and Practice of Medicine* was first published in 1892.
2. Thomas Carlyle, "Signs of the Times," in *Critical and Miscellaneous Essays: Collected and Republished* (Boston: Dana Estes and Charles E. Lauriat, 1884), 1:462; Dale Carnegie, *How to Stop Worrying and Start Living: Time-Tested Methods for Conquering Worry,* rev. ed. (New York: Pocket Books, 2004), 3.
3. William Osler, *A Way of Life: An Address to Yale Students Sunday Evening, April 20th, 1913* (London: Constable, 1913), https://archive.org/details/awayoflifeanaddr00osleuoft/page/n5.
4. Osler, *A Way of Life,* 14. I discovered these words in Dale Carnegie's classic book *How to Stop Worrying and Start Living,* 4.
5. Osler, *A Way of Life,* 29.
6. Osler, *A Way of Life,* 23.
7. Osler, *A Way of Life,* 22–23; Carnegie, *How to Stop Worrying,* 3–4.
8. Tony Campolo, "If I Should Wake Before I Die," Preaching Today, www.preachingtoday.com/sermons/sermons/2005/august/124.html.
9. Steve Bradt, "Wandering Mind Not a Happy Mind," Harvard Gazette, November 11, 2010, https://news.harvard.edu/gazette/story/2010/11/wandering-mind-not-a-happy-mind.
10. Frank C. Laubach, *Letters by a Modern Mystic* (London: Society for Promoting Christian Knowledge, 2011), 15.
11. Psalm 90:12.
12. "Emmitt Smith," Pro Football Hall of Fame, www.profootballhof.com/players/emmitt-smith/biography.
13. Matthew 6:11, ESV.
14. Osler, *A Way of Life,* 18–19.
15. Matthew 6:12.
16. Matthew 6:13.
17. Matthew 6:11, ESV.
18. Exodus 16:19–20.

19. Ephesians 4:26.
20. Lamentations 3:22–23.
21. Luke 9:23.
22. Psalm 118:24.
23. Genesis 1:5, ESV.
24. Ashira Prossack, "This Year, Don't Set New Year's Resolutions," *Forbes,* December 31, 2018, www.forbes.com/sites/ashira prossack1/2018/12/31/goals-not-resolutions/#12aea983879a.

PART 1: BURY DEAD YESTERDAYS

1. Victoria, quoted in Christopher Hibbert, *Queen Victoria: A Personal History* (Cambridge, MA: Da Capo, 2001), 123.
2. Peter Scazzero, *Emotionally Healthy Spirituality: It's Impossible to Be Spiritually Mature While Remaining Emotionally Immature,* rev. ed. (Grand Rapids, MI: Zondervan, 2017), 121.
3. Sam Cooke, "A Change Is Gonna Come," *Ain't That Good News,* RCA Victor, 1964.
4. Job 2:13.

HABIT 1: FLIP THE SCRIPT

1. Eric Metaxas, *Martin Luther: The Man Who Rediscovered God and Changed the World* (New York: Viking, 2017), 1.
2. Maynard Solomon, *Mozart: A Life* (New York: HarperPerennial, 1996), 282.
3. Mark 3:17.
4. Revelation 2:17, ESV.
5. Numbers 6:24–27.

CHAPTER 1: SIGNATURE STORY

1. Winfield M. Thompson and Thomas W. Lawson, *The Lawson History of the America's Cup: A Record of Fifty Years* (Boston: printed by the author, 1902), 29.
2. "America's Cup Win," National Museum of Australia, www.nma .gov.au/defining-moments/resources/americas-cup-win; "History of the America's Cup," AmericasCup.com, www.americascup.com /en/history.
3. Richard Bach, *Jonathan Livingston Seagull: A Story,* complete ed. (New York: Scribner, 2014), 56.

4. Stephen R. Covey, *The 7 Habits of Highly Effective People: Powerful Lessons in Personal Change,* rev. ed. (New York: Simon & Schuster, 2020), 109.

5. Jack Canfield and Mark Victor Hansen, *The Aladdin Factor: How to Ask for What You Want—and Get It* (New York: Berkley, 1995), 76.

6. Bo Eason, *There's No Plan B for Your A-Game: Be the Best in the World at What You Do* (New York: St. Martin's, 2019), 1.

7. Hebrews 11:1.

8. Eason, *There's No Plan B,* 2.

9. Hebrews 12:2.

10. John C. Maxwell, *3 Things Successful People Do: The Road Map That Will Change Your Life* (Nashville: Nelson Books, 2016), 93.

11. "LifePlan," Paterson Center, https://patersoncenter.com/lifeplan.

12. Matthew 19:26.

13. Tim Ferriss, quoted in Rachel Gregg, "Passion and Practice: Tim Ferriss & Neil Strauss's Tips for Better Writing," *CreativeLive Blog,* www.creativelive.com/blog/tim-ferriss-neil-strauss-writing-advice.

14. Bill Peschel, "Ingmar Bergman Quote About Filmmaking," Peschel Press, November 9, 2018, https://peschelpress.com/ingmar-bergman-quote-about-filmmaking.

15. "Emil Zátopek: The Man Who Changed Running," *Runner's World,* September 16, 2016, www.runnersworld.com/uk/training/a775206/emil-zatopek-the-man-who-changed-running.

16. Deuteronomy 1:2.

17. Numbers 11:5, AMPC.

18. Joshua 5:9.

19. Chris Myers Asch and George Derek Musgrove, *Chocolate City: A History of Race and Democracy in the Nation's Capital* (Chapel Hill, NC: University of North Carolina Press, 2017).

20. Martin Luther King Jr., "I Have a Dream" (speech, March on Washington, Washington, DC, August 28, 1963), 1, www.archives.gov/files/press/exhibits/dream-speech.pdf.

21. Karl Barth, quoted in "Barth in Retirement," *Time,* May 31, 1963, http://content.time.com/time/magazine/article/0,9171,896838,00.html.

22. 2 Corinthians 5:17.

23. Psalm 17:8.

24. Ephesians 2:10, KJV.

25. Romans 8:37.

Chapter 2: Ambidexterity

1. Ashlee Vance, *Elon Musk: Tesla, SpaceX, and the Quest for a Fantastic Future,* rev. ed. (New York: Ecco, 2017), 26–28.

2. Vance, *Elon Musk,* 30.

3. 1 Chronicles 12:2, NLT.

4. Anders Ericsson and Robert Pool, *Peak: Secrets from the New Science of Expertise* (New York: Mariner Books, 2017), 14, 109–10.

5. Ericsson and Pool, *Peak,* 39–40, 99–100.

6. Ericsson and Pool, *Peak,* 113.

7. Judges 3:15, AMPC.

8. 2 Corinthians 12:9.

9. Roger Kahn, *The Boys of Summer: The Classic Narrative of Growing Up Within Shouting Distance of Ebbets Field, Covering the Jackie Robinson Dodgers, and What's Happened to Everybody Since* (New York: HarperPerennial, 2006), 224.

10. Kahn, *The Boys of Summer,* 241.

11. Maria Millett, "Challenge Your Negative Thoughts," MSU Extension, March 31, 2017, www.canr.msu.edu/news/challenge_your _negative_thoughts.

12. Chris Landers, "The Story of Gaylord Perry, the Moon Landing and a Most Unlikely Home Run," Cut4, July 20, 2017, www.mlb .com/cut4/gaylord-perry-hits-home-run-just-minutes-after -neil-armstrong-moon-landing-c2433.

13. Attributed to Henry Ford; see "Whether You Believe You Can Do a Thing or Not, You Are Right," Quote Investigator, February 3, 2015, https://quoteinvestigator.com/2015/02/03/you-can.

14. Malcolm Gladwell, *David and Goliath: Underdogs, Misfits, and the Art of Battling Giants* (New York: Little, Brown, 2013), 11.

15. 1 Samuel 17:7.

16. 1 Samuel 17:33, NLT.

17. 1 Samuel 17:37, ESV.

18. Eric Barker, *Barking Up the Wrong Tree: The Surprising Science Behind Why Everything You Know About Success Is (Mostly) Wrong* (New York: HarperCollins, 2017), 26.

19. Dean Keith Simonton, *Origins of Genius: Darwinian Perspectives on Creativity* (New York: Oxford University Press, 1999), 115–16.

20. John 1:46, ESV.

21. Vance, *Elon Musk,* 38, 40–41.

22. "Children Benefit If They Know About Their Relatives, Study

Finds," Emory University, March 3, 2010, http://shared.web.emory
.edu/emory/news/releases/2010/03/children-benefit-if-they
-know-about-their-relatives-study-finds.html#.XqX_x5opCVo.

HABIT 2: KISS THE WAVE

1. Eli Meixler, "Today Is Wilder Penfield's 127th Birthday. Here's
   Why Google Is Honoring Him," *Time*, January 26, 2018, https://
   time.com/5119901/wilder-penfield-127th-birthday.

CHAPTER 3: THE OBSTACLE IS THE WAY

1. Frederick Treves, quoted in Jenny Paschall, "How the 'Elephant
   Man' Actually Looked: Staggering Pics Show Skeleton and Post-
   Mortem Bust," Express, September 3, 2015, www.express.co.uk
   /news/weird/602782/Elephant-Man-looked-Staggering-images
   -skeleton-post-mortem.
2. Frederick Treves, *The Elephant Man and Other Reminiscences*
   (London: Cassell, 1923), 22.
3. Treves, *Elephant Man*, 22.
4. Treves, *Elephant Man*, 24.
5. Treves, *Elephant Man*, 17.
6. "6 Quotes Spurgeon Didn't Say," Spurgeon Center, August 8,
   2017, www.spurgeon.org/resource-library/blog-entries/6-quotes
   -spurgeon-didnt-say. (But were often attributed to Spurgeon.)
7. Mark 4:39, KJV.
8. Proverbs 17:22, KJV.
9. John Piper, *Don't Waste Your Cancer* (Wheaton, IL: Crossway,
   2011).
10. Proverbs 3:33, KJV.
11. Thomas H. Holmes and Richard H. Rahe, "The Social Readjust-
    ment Rating Scale," *Journal of Psychosomatic Research* 11, no. 2
    (1967): 213–18, www.sciencedirect.com/science/article/abs/pii
    /0022399967900104?via%3Dihub.
12. C. H. Spurgeon, "The Christian's Heaviness and Rejoicing" (ser-
    mon, Surrey Gardens Music Hall, London, November 7, 1858),
    www.spurgeon.org/resource-library/sermons/the-christians
    -heaviness-and-rejoicing#flipbook.
13. Andrew Solomon, *The Noonday Demon: An Atlas of Depression*
    (New York: Scribner, 2014), 16.

14. Elisabeth Kübler-Ross and David Kessler, *On Grief and Grieving: Finding the Meaning of Grief Through the Five Stages of Loss* (New York: Scribner, 2014), 7.

15. 1 Thessalonians 4:13.

16. Kevin Fitzpatrick, "Stephen Colbert's Outlook on Grief Moved Anderson Cooper to Tears," *Vanity Fair,* August 16, 2019, www.vanityfair.com/hollywood/2019/08/colbert-anderson-cooper-father-grief-tears.

17. Stephen Colbert, quoted in Fitzpatrick, "Stephen Colbert's Outlook on Grief."

18. "Joseph Merrick," Wikiquote, last modified January 13, 2018, https://en.wikiquote.org/wiki/Joseph_Merrick.

19. C. H. Spurgeon, *The Soul-Winner; or, How to Lead Sinners to the Saviour* (New York: Revell, 1895), 286.

20. Adapted from Reinhold Niebuhr; see Fred R. Shapiro, "Who Wrote the Serenity Prayer?," *Yale Alumni Magazine,* July/August 2008, https://yalealumnimagazine.com/articles/2143.

21. Wikipedia, s.v. "Serenity Prayer," last modified June 20, 2020, 17:45, https://en.wikipedia.org/wiki/Serenity_Prayer.

22. Frederick Buechner, *The Sacred Journey: A Memoir of Early Days* (New York: HarperSanFrancisco, 1982), 46.

23. Kathleen Norris, *Amazing Grace: A Vocabulary of Faith* (New York: Riverhead Books, 1998), 71.

24. Martin Luther, "A Mighty Fortress Is Our God," trans. Frederick H. Hedge, 1852, public domain.

25. John 19:30.

26. Luke 9:23.

Chapter 4: Postimagining

1. M. Craig Barnes, *The Pastor as Minor Poet: Texts and Subtexts in the Ministerial Life* (Grand Rapids, MI: Eerdmans, 2009), 46.

2. *Jerry Maguire,* directed by Cameron Crowe (Culver City, CA: TriStar Pictures, 1996).

3. Leonardo Da Vinci, *Leonardo Da Vinci's Note-Books,* trans. Edward McCurdy (London: Duckworth, 1906), 53.

4. Bessel van der Kolk, *The Body Keeps the Score: Brain, Mind, and Body in the Healing of Trauma* (New York: Penguin Books, 2014), 146.

5. John 5:6.

6. John 5:14.

7. Steve Jobs, quoted in Philip Michaels, "Jobs: OS 9 Is Dead, Long Live OS X," *Macworld*, April 30, 2002, www.macworld.com /article/1001445/06wwdc.html.
8. Genesis 35:4.
9. Genesis 12:6–7.
10. Matthew 26:34, ESV.
11. Revelation 12:10.
12. 1 Peter 5:8.
13. Matthew 5:44.
14. Luke 6:27.
15. Luke 6:28.
16. Matthew 5:41, ESV.
17. Matthew 5:39, ESV.
18. John 21:3.
19. John 21:15.
20. John 21:4, NLT.
21. Lamentations 3:22–23, ESV.

Part 2: Win the Day

1. Acts 1:12–14.
2. *Stranger than Fiction*, directed by Marc Forster (Culver City, CA: Columbia Pictures, 2006).
3. Psalm 50:10.
4. Joshua 3:5.

Habit 3: Eat the Frog

1. "Eat a Live Frog Every Morning, and Nothing Worse Will Happen to You the Rest of the Day," Quote Investigator, April 3, 2013, https://quoteinvestigator.com/2013/04/03/eat-frog.

Chapter 5: Habit Stacking

1. William H. McRaven, *Make Your Bed: Little Things That Can Change Your Life . . . and Maybe the World* (New York: Grand Central, 2017), 1.
2. "Bio," Twyla Tharp Dance Foundation, www.twylatharp.org/bio.
3. Twyla Tharp, *The Creative Habit: Learn It and Use It for Life* (New York: Simon & Schuster, 2006), 15.
4. Tharp, *The Creative Habit*, 14.
5. Tharp, *The Creative Habit*, 14–15.

6. This sequence appears during each of the six creation days in Genesis 1.

7. Ephesians 4:26, ESV.

8. Oscar Hammerstein II, "Oh, What a Beautiful Morning," *Oklahoma!*, 1943.

9. Joseph Epstein, "Think You Have a Book in You? Think Again," *New York Times*, September 28, 2002, www.nytimes.com/2002/09/28/opinion/think-you-have-a-book-in-you-think-again.html.

10. McRaven, *Make Your Bed*, 111.

11. R. A. Torrey, quoted in George Sweeting and Donald Sweeting, *Lessons from the Life of Moody* (Chicago: Moody, 1989), 129.

12. Eben Pagan, quoted in Hal Elrod, *The Miracle Morning* (Austin, TX: Hal Elrod International, 2017), 37.

13. Blake Stilwell, "Here's What NASA Says Is the Perfect Length for a Power Nap," Business Insider, March 25, 2019, www.businessinsider.com/nasa-research-found-the-perfect-length-for-a-power-nap-2019-3.

14. Ryan Swanson, *The Strenuous Life: Theodore Roosevelt and the Making of the American Athlete* (New York: Diversion Books, 2019), 16.

15. Deuteronomy 6:7, NLT.

16. Deuteronomy 6:7.

17. Sarah Berger, "These Are the States with the Longest and Shortest Commutes—How Does Yours Stack Up?," CNBC, February 23, 2018, www.cnbc.com/2018/02/22/study-states-with-the-longest-and-shortest-commutes.html.

18. Psalm 37:26, AMPC.

19. Psalm 119:164, NLT.

20. Psalm 57:8.

21. Daniel 6:10.

22. Mark 11:12–14.

23. Lewis Carroll, *Through the Looking-Glass and What Alice Found There* (Philadelphia: Henry Altemus, 1897), 48, 50.

24. Rosemary K. M. Sword and Philip Zimbardo, "Hurry Sickness," *Psychology Today*, February 9, 2013, www.psychologytoday.com/us/blog/the-time-cure/201302/hurry-sickness.

25. Eugene H. Peterson, *Under the Unpredictable Plant: An Exploration in Vocational Holiness* (Grand Rapids, MI: Eerdmans, 1994), 50.

26. Henri J. M. Nouwen, *The Genesee Diary: Report from a Trappist Monastery* (New York: Doubleday, 1981), 14.

27. Howard Leventhal, Robert Singer, and Susan Jones, "Effects of Fear and Specificity of Recommendation upon Attitudes and Behavior," *Journal of Personality and Social Psychology* 2, no. 1 (1965): 20–29.

CHAPTER 6: THE MUNDANITY OF EXCELLENCE

1. "Electrified," David Blaine, https://davidblaine.com/electrified.

2. Jodi Smith, "David Blaine's Grossest, Most Disturbing Magic Tricks," Ranker, May 23, 2018, www.ranker.com/list/grossest -david-blaine-magic-tricks/jodi-smith.

3. David Blaine, "How I Held My Breath for 17 Minutes," TED, October 2009, www.ted.com/talks/david_blaine_how_i_held_my _breath_for_17_minutes/transcript?language=en.

4. Friedrich Nietzsche, *Human, All Too Human: A Book for Free Spirits,* trans. R. J. Hollingdale (Cambridge: Cambridge University Press, 1996), 80.

5. Friedrich Nietzsche, *Human, All-Too-Human: A Book for Free Spirits,* trans. Paul V. Cohn (New York: Macmillan, 1913), 100.

6. Angela Duckworth, *Grit: The Power of Passion and Perseverance* (New York: Scribner, 2016), 39.

7. Blaine, "How I Held My Breath."

8. Daniel F. Chambliss, "The Mundanity of Excellence: An Ethnographic Report on Stratification and Olympic Swimmers," *Sociological Theory* 7, no. 1 (1989): 78, https://academics.hamilton.edu /documents/themundanityofexcellence.pdf.

9. Quoted in John Livesay, "The Success Secret Leaders Can Borrow from Michael Phelps," *Forbes,* February 19, 2019, www.forbes.com /sites/forbescoachescouncil/2019/02/19/the-success-secret -leaders-can-borrow-from-michael-phelps/#549a693262db.

10. Exodus 20:8.

11. Chambliss, "The Mundanity of Excellence," 81.

12. Ed Mylett and Phil Mickelson, "Visualize Your Victory W/ Phil Mickelson," May 19, 2020, in *The Ed Mylett Show,* podcast, https:// podcastgang.com/podcast/ed-mylett-show/310890342872254.

13. Will Koehrsen, "The Mundanity of Excellence: Talent Does Not Determine Success and Why That Terrifies People," Medium, August 6, 2019, https://medium.com/@williamkoehrsen/the

-mundanity-of-excellence-talent-does-not-determine-success
-and-why-that-terrifies-people-146a67e69f71.

14. Horst Schulze, *Excellence Wins: A No-Nonsense Guide to Be-coming the Best in a World of Compromise* (Grand Rapids, MI: Zondervan, 2019), 19–21.

15. William H. McRaven, *Make Your Bed: Little Things That Can Change Your Life . . . and Maybe the World* (New York: Grand Central, 2017), 111.

16. Earl Nightingale, quoted in Patrick Byron, "An Extra Hour Learn-ing per Day Will Bring Success Your Way," Medium, February 15, 2019, https://medium.com/swlh/an-extra-hour-learning-per-day-will-bring-success-your-way-6ac69ac47fbb.

17. Rowdy Gaines, quoted in Duckworth, *Grit*, 132.

18. Malcolm Gladwell, *Outliers: The Story of Success* (New York: Little, Brown, 2008), 249.

19. Thomas H. Palmer, *The Teacher's Manual: Being an Exposition of an Efficient and Economical System of Education, Suited to the Wants of a Free People* (Boston: Marsh, Capen, Lyon, and Webb, 1840), 223.

20. Marshall Goldsmith, *Triggers: Creating Behavior That Lasts, Be-coming the Person You Want to Be* (New York: Crown Business, 2015), 9–10.

21. London Philharmonic Orchestra and David Parry, *The 50 Great-est Pieces of Classical Music*, X5 Music Group, 2009.

22. Adam Grant, *Originals: How Non-Conformists Move the World* (New York: Penguin Books, 2017), 36.

23. Wikipedia, s.v. "false positives and false negatives," last modi-fied April 11, 2020, 23:21, https://en.wikipedia.org/wiki/False_positives_and_false_negatives.

24. Grant, *Originals*, 34–35.

25. *Finding Nemo*, directed by Andrew Stanton (Emeryville, CA: Pixar Animation Studios, 2003).

26. George Bernard Shaw, *Mrs. Warren's Profession: An Unpleasant Play* (New York: Brentano's, 1914), 41.

Habit 4: Fly the Kite

1. "Facts About Niagara Falls," Niagara Falls State Park, www.niagara fallsstatepark.com/niagara-falls-state-park/amazing-niagara -facts.

2. Michelle Ann Kratts, "The Cementation of the Dead; the Story of

Theodore Graves Hulett's Most Curious Work in Oakwood Cemetery," Oakwood Cemetery, March 15, 2012, https://oakwood niagara.org/kratts-korner/2012/3/15/the-cementation-of-the -dead-the-story-of-theodore-graves-hul.html.

3. M. Robinson, "The Kite That Bridged a River," 2005, www.kite history.com/Miscellaneous/Homan_Walsh.htm.

4. Quoted in "Niagara Suspension Bridge," *American Railroad Journal* 4, no. 7 (February 12, 1848): 98.

5. Zechariah 4:10, NLT.

Chapter 7: Make Each Day a Masterpiece

1. *Encyclopaedia Britannica*, s.v. "John Wooden," www.britannica .com/biography/John-Wooden; "The Journey," John Wooden, www.coachwooden.com/the-journey; Mike Penner, "99 Things About John Wooden," *Los Angeles Times*, October 14, 2009, www .latimes.com/archives/la-xpm-2009-oct-14-sp-john-wooden14 -story.html.

2. Sid Hartman, "Wooden Missed Chance to Coach at U," *Star Tribune*, June 5, 2010, www.startribune.com/wooden-missed-chance -to-coach-for-gophers/95702419; "John Wooden: Preparing for UCLA, Arriving in Westwood," UCLABruins.com, https://ucla bruins.com/sports/2013/4/17/208274581.aspx.

3. Paul Putz, "John Wooden's Homespun Creed Was Not So Homespun," Slate, May 17, 2017, https://slate.com/culture/2017 /05/john-woodens-seven-point-creed-came-from-a-1931 -magazine-article.html.

4. I'm not sure who developed this metaphor, but Stephen Covey preached it well. See Stephen R. Covey, *The 7 Habits of Highly Effective People: Powerful Lessons in Personal Change*, rev. ed. (New York: Simon & Schuster, 2020), 112.

5. Dave Ramsey, *The Total Money Makeover: A Proven Plan for Financial Fitness* (Nashville: Thomas Nelson, 2009), 31.

6. Genesis 1:10, 12, 18, 21, 25.

7. Genesis 1:31, ESV.

8. "Blood Vessels," Franklin Institute, www.fi.edu/heart/blood -vessels.

9. Barry Starr, "A Long and Winding DNA," KQED, February 2, 2009, www.kqed.org/quest/1219/a-long-and-winding-dna.

10. "Albert Einstein," Wikiquote, last modified June 5, 2020, https:// en.wikiquote.org/wiki/Albert_Einstein.

11. Judith Viorst, *Alexander and the Terrible, Horrible, No Good, Very Bad Day* (New York: Atheneum, 1972).

12. Theodore Roosevelt, "Foreword to *A Book-Lover's Holidays in the Open,* and On an East African Ranch," in *The Book of Naturalists: An Anthology of the Best Natural History,* ed. William Beebe (Princeton, NJ: Princeton University Press, 1988), 234.

13. Genesis 1:3.

14. Proverbs 6:6.

15. John Wooden, in John Wooden and Steve Jamison, *The Wisdom of Wooden: My Century on and off the Court* (New York: McGraw-Hill, 2010).

16. "Sporting News Honors Wooden," ESPN, July 29, 2009, www .espn.com/mens-college-basketball/news/story?id=4365068.

17. Bill Walton, *Back from the Dead* (New York: Simon & Schuster Paperbacks, 2017), 70.

18. John Wooden, *Wooden: A Lifetime of Observations and Reflections on and off the Court* (New York: McGraw-Hill, 1997), 63.

19. Luke 16:10, NLT.

20. 1 Kings 7:20, NLT.

21. Dorothy L. Sayers, "Why Work?," in *Letters to a Diminished Church: Passionate Arguments for the Relevance of Christian Doctrine* (Nashville: W Publishing, 2004), 132.

22. Colossians 3:23.

23. Martin Luther King Jr., "Facing the Challenge of a New Age" (speech, NAACP Emancipation Day Rally, Atlanta, GA, January 1, 1957), in *The Papers of Martin Luther King Jr.,* ed. Clayborne Carson, vol. 4, *Symbol of the Movement: January 1957—December 1958* (Berkeley: University of California Press, 2000), 79.

24. Kate Streit, "15 Facts You Never Knew About Fred Rogers," Simplemost, April 23, 2018, www.simplemost.com/mister-rogers -neighborhood-facts.

25. John Wooden, quoted in John C. Maxwell, *Today Matters: 12 Daily Practices to Guarantee Tomorrow's Success* (New York: Warner Faith, 2004), 34.

26. Alan Stein Jr., Cadre Con Conference, May 2018.

27. Tony Manfred, "16 Examples of Kobe Bryant's Insane Work Ethic," Business Insider, February 23, 2013, www.businessinsider .com/kobe-bryant-work-ethic-2013-2#he-says-he-taught-himself -to-play-beethovens-moonlight-sonata-on-piano-by-ear-11.

28. Kobe Bryant, quoted in Paul Kennedy Lintag, "So What Does

Mamba Mentality Really Mean?," ABS-CBN Sports, June 25, 2016, https://sports.abs-cbn.com/basketball/news/2016/06/25/so-mamba-mentality-really-mean-12684.

29. Kobe Bryant, "Dear Basketball," Players' Tribune, November 29, 2015, www.theplayerstribune.com/en-us/articles/dear-basketball.

30. Kobe Bryant, quoted in Scott Davis and Connor Perrett, "Kobe Bryant Was Known for His Intense Work Ethic, Here Are 24 Examples," Business Insider, January 26, 2020, www.businessinsider.com/kobe-bryant-insane-work-ethic-2013-8.

31. Matthew 25:23.

Chapter 8: Kaizen

1. Samuel Smiles, *Self-Help; with Illustrations of Character and Conduct* (London: John Murray, 1859).

2. Jeffrey K. Liker, *The Toyota Way: 14 Management Principles from the World's Greatest Manufacturer* (New York: McGraw-Hill, 2004), 16.

3. "Toyota Net Worth," Celebrity Net Worth, www.celebritynetworth.com/richest-businessmen/companies/toyotas-net-worth.

4. Exodus 23:30.

5. Exodus 23:29.

6. Exodus 23:30.

7. Exodus 23:29.

8. This formula combines ideas acquired from a variety of books including these: David Epstein, *Range: Why Generalists Triumph in a Specialized World* (New York: Riverhead Books, 2019); Anders Ericsson and Robert Pool, *Peak: Secrets from the New Science of Expertise* (New York: Mariner Books, 2017); and James Clear, *Atomic Habits: An Easy & Proven Way to Build Good Habits & Break Bad Ones* (New York: Avery, 2018).

9. "Margaret Thatcher," Goodreads, www.goodreads.com/quotes/66737-look-at-a-day-when-you-are-supremely-satisfied-at.

10. Robert A. Bjork, "Institutional Impediments to Effective Training," epilogue to *Learning, Remembering, Believing: Enhanced Human Performance,* ed. Daniel Druckman and Robert A. Bjork (Washington, DC: National Academy Press, 1994), 299.

11. Wikipedia, s.v. "desirable difficulty," last modified June 3, 2020, 18:08, https://en.wikipedia.org/wiki/Desirable_difficulty.

12. James 1:2–4.

13. Psalm 84:7.

14. Quoted in Richard Askwith, *Today We Die a Little!* (New York: Bold Type, 2016), 136.

15. Emil Zátopek, quoted in Rick Broadbent, *Endurance: The Extraordinary Life and Times of Emil Zátopek* (London: John Wisden, 2016), 218.

16. Emil Zátopek, quoted in Askwith, *Today We Die a Little!*, 199.

17. Emil Zátopek, quoted in Askwith, *Today We Die a Little!*, 293.

18. Luke 9:23.

19. Blake Finney, "Washington Nationals' 'Go 1-0 today' Mantra More Important than Ever with World Series Lead," SBNation Federal Baseball, October 25, 2019, www.federalbaseball.com /2019/10/25/20931340/washington-nationals-go-1-0-today -mantra-more-important-than-ever-world-series-lead.

PART 3: IMAGINE UNBORN TOMORROWS

1. 2 Corinthians 10:5.

2. Ephesians 2:10, BSB.

3. Hayim Nahman Bialik and Yehoshua Hana Ravnitzy, eds., *The Book of Legends—Sefer Ha-Aggadah: Legends from the Talmud and Midrash,* trans., William G. Braude (New York: Schocken, 1992), 16.

4. Ephesians 3:20.

HABIT 5: CUT THE ROPE

1. Matthew 14:25–32.

2. Nick Paumgarten, "Up and Then Down: The Lives of Elevators," *New Yorker,* last modified July 28, 2014, www.newyorker.com /magazine/2008/04/21/up-and-then-down.

3. "Escalators and Moving Walks," Otis, www.otis.com/en/id /products/escalators-moving-walks.

CHAPTER 9: THE ADJACENT POSSIBLE

1. Neal Bascomb, in "Skyscrapers: An Upward Journey," *Trailblazers,* October 22, 2019, www.delltechnologies.com/en-us /perspectives/podcasts-trailblazers-s04-e03.

2. Walter Chrysler, quoted by Bascomb in "Skyscrapers."

3. Proverbs 27:1.

4. Stuart Kauffman, in "The Adjacent Possible: A Talk with Stuart Kauffman," Edge.org, November 9, 2003, www.edge.org /conversation/stuart_a_kauffman-the-adjacent-possible.

5. Ephesians 4:26.

6. Acts 16:7–10.

7. Mark 12:30–31.

8. Matthew 5–7.

9. Philippians 4:13.

10. John 2:1–10.

11. John 6:35; 8:12; 10:9, esv; 10:11; 11:25; 14:6, nlt; 15:5.

12. John 6:1–13.

13. John 9:1–7.

14. Genesis 1:3; John 11:1–44, kjv.

15. Exodus 14:26–31.

16. 2 Kings 6:1–7.

17. Joshua 10:12–14.

18. Steven Johnson, "The Genius of the Tinkerer," *Wall Street Journal,* September 25, 2010, www.wsj.com/articles/SB10001424052 7487039893045755503730101860838.

19. Philippians 1:6.

20. Romans 8:37.

21. Hebrews 11:1.

22. Dennis Hevesi, "Off the Brooklyn Bridge and into History," *New York Times,* July 23, 1986, www.nytimes.com/1986/07/23 /nyregion/off-the-brooklyn-bridge-and-into-history.html.

CHAPTER 10: THE GRAND GESTURE

1. Barry M. Staw, "Knee-Deep in the Big Muddy: A Study of Escalating Commitment to a Chosen Course of Action," *Organizational Behavior and Human Performance* 16, no. 1 (1976): 27–44.

2. Matthew 6:27.

3. J. K. Rowling, quoted in Cal Newport, *Deep Work: Rules for Focused Success in a Distracted World* (New York: Grand Central, 2016), 122.

4. "Fastest-Selling Book of Fiction in 24 Hours," Guinness World Records, www.guinnessworldrecords.com/world-records/fastest -selling-book-of-fiction-in-24-hours; Motoko Rich, "Record First-Day Sales for Last 'Harry Potter' Book," *New York Times,* www.nytimes.com/2007/07/22/books/22cnd-potter.html;

" 'Harry Potter and the Deathly Hallows' Breaks Records," Fox News, July 24, 2007, www.foxnews.com/story/harry-potter-and -the-deathly-hallows-breaks-records.

5. Newport, *Deep Work,* 122.
6. Joshua 6:2–5; 1 Kings 19:21; Ezekiel 4:4–5; Matthew 2:1–2; Matthew 4:18–20; Acts 19:17–19.
7. Matthew 27:24, AMPC.
8. William Ellery Channing, quoted in Barbara L. Packer, *The Transcendentalists* (Athens: University of Georgia Press, 2007), 183.
9. Henry D. Thoreau, *Walden* (Boston: Houghton, Mifflin, 1897), 143.
10. Albert Einstein, quoted in William Miller, "Old Man's Advice to Youth: 'Never Lost a Holy Curiosity,' " *Life,* May 2, 1955, 64.
11. Matthew 25:23.
12. Benjamin Franklin, *The Way to Wealth* (London: W. and T. Darton, 1810), 14.
13. Mark Twain, quoted in "Never Put Off till Tomorrow What You Can Do the Day After Tomorrow Just as Well," Quote Investigator, https://quoteinvestigator.com/2013/01/17/put-off.
14. Frederick Buechner, *The Alphabet of Grace* (New York: Harper Collins, 1989), 39.
15. Buechner, *The Alphabet of Grace,* 40.
16. Galatians 2:20.
17. Buechner, *The Alphabet of Grace,* 40.
18. James 4:17, ESV.
19. Joshua 6:1–2.
20. John 6:5, AMPC.
21. John 6:6, AMPC.
22. Psalm 13:1, ESV.
23. Deuteronomy 24:15.
24. Genesis 17:26, AMPC.
25. Hebrews 3:15.

HABIT 6: WIND THE CLOCK

1. David McCullough, "Simon Willard's Clock," in *The American Spirit: Who We Are and What We Stand For* (New York: Simon & Schuster, 2017), 14.
2. 2 Peter 3:8.
3. Ephesians 2:10.
4. Proverbs 16:9.

5. John Piper, *Don't Waste Your Life* (Wheaton, IL: Crossway Books, 2007), 19.
6. McCullough, "Simon Willard's Clock," in *The American Spirit*, 12.
7. Ephesians 5:16, KJV.
8. Elizabeth Barrett Browning, *Aurora Leigh: A Poem* (Chicago: Academy Chicago, 1979), 265.

CHAPTER 11: COUNTERCLOCKWISE

1. Philip Goldberg, *The Babinski Reflex: And 70 Other Useful and Amusing Metaphors from Science, Psychology, Business, Sports . . . and Everyday Life* (Los Angeles: Jeremy P. Tarcher, 1990), 198–99.
2. Psalm 118:24, ESV.
3. "The Digital Universe of Opportunities: Rich Data and the Increasing Value of the Internet of Things," EMC, April 2014, www.emc.com/leadership/digital-universe/2014iview/executive-summary.htm.
4. Rudi Dalman, "The Real Cost of Interruptions at Work," People HR, May 12, 2016, www.peoplehr.com/blog/2016/05/12/the-real-cost-of-interruptions-at-work.
5. Saima Salim, "How Much Time Do You Spend on Social Media? Research Says 142 Minutes per Day," Digital Information World, January 4, 2019, www.digitalinformationworld.com/2019/01/how-much-time-do-people-spend-social-media-infographic.html.
6. Brandon G. Donnelly, "People in Big Cities Walk Faster," Smart Cities Dive, www.smartcitiesdive.com/ex/sustainablecitiescollective/people-big-cities-walk-faster/1022061.
7. Wisława Szymborska, "The Three Oddest Words," Nobel Prize, www.nobelprize.org/prizes/literature/1996/szymborska/25558-poetry-1996-7.
8. Robert Herrick, "To the Virgins, to Make Much of Time," Poetry Foundation, www.poetryfoundation.org/poems/46546/to-the-virgins-to-make-much-of-time.
9. Ellen J. Langer, *Counterclockwise: Mindful Health and the Power of Possibility* (New York: Ballantine Books, 2009), jacket.
10. Langer, *Counterclockwise*, 5.
11. Langer, *Counterclockwise*, 8–9.
12. Joshua 14:11, AMPC.
13. Langer, *Counterclockwise*, 10.
14. Lauren F. Friedman, "A Radical Experiment Tried to Make

Old People Young Again—and the Results Were Astonishing," *Business Insider*, April 6, 2015, www.businessinsider.com/ellen -langers-reversing-aging-experiment-2015-4.

15. Langer, *Counterclockwise*, 11.
16. Proverbs 23:7, KJV.
17. Genesis 39:10, NLT.
18. Dale Carnegie, *How to Stop Worrying and Start Living: Time-Tested Methods for Conquering Worry*, rev. ed. (New York: Pocket Books, 2004), 101.
19. Joseph Dispenza, quoted in *What the Bleep Do We Know!?*, directed by William Arntz, Betsy Chasse, and Mark Vincente (Los Angeles: 20th Century Fox, 2004).
20. Matthew 18:3.
21. Mitch Albom, *Tuesdays with Morrie: An Old Man, a Young Man, and Life's Greatest Lesson* (New York: Broadway Books, 2017), 118.
22. Albom, *Tuesdays with Morrie*, 118.
23. Albom, *Tuesdays with Morrie*, 120–21.
24. Numbers 13:30, AMPC.
25. Joshua 14:12.
26. Elise Boulding, quoted in Richard Fisher, "The Perils of Short-Termism: Civilisation's Greatest Threat," BBC, January 9, 2019, www.bbc.com/future/article/20190109-the-perils-of-short -termism-civilisations-greatest-threat.
27. Shirley Showalter, "The 200-Year Present: A Way to Lengthen Your Days," *Discover the Power of Writing Your Story (blog)*, March 1, 2018, https://shirleyshowalter.com/the-200-year-present-a-way -to-lengthen-your-days.

Chapter 12: Persistence Hunting

1. Ed Young, "It's a Myth That Cheetahs Overheat While Hunting," *National Geographic*, July 23, 2013, www.nationalgeographic .com/science/phenomena/2013/07/23/its-a-myth-that-cheetahs -overheat-while-hunting.
2. Frederick Schwatka, quoted in Davy Crockett, "The Tarahumara Ultrarunners," Ultrarunning History, July 3, 2019, http://ultra runninghistory.com/tarahumara.
3. Crockett, "The Tarahumara Ultrarunners."
4. Quoted in Crockett, "The Tarahumara Ultrarunners."
5. Crockett, "The Tarahumara Ultrarunners."
6. Frederick Schwatka, *In the Land of Cave and Cliff Dwellers* (New

York: Cassell, 1893), 239, https://babel.hathitrust.org/cgi/pt?id =loc.ark:/13960/t2q53d123&view=1up&seq=257.

7. Will Smith, interview by Tavis Smiley, "Will Smith Segment on Tavis Smiley," video, 6:23, www.youtube.com/watch?v=VH6mPe QfRLY.

8. Louis Liebenberg, quoted in Christopher McDougall, *Born to Run: A Hidden Tribe, Superathletes, and the Greatest Race the World Has Never Seen* (New York: Vintage Books, 2011), 236.

9. 1 Samuel 14:6.

10. Esther 2:21.

11. Acts 10:3.

12. James Clear, "Rome Wasn't Built in a Day, but They Were Laying Bricks Every Hour," James Clear, https://jamesclear.com/lay-a -brick.

13. Quoted in Stephen J. Kraus, *Psychological Foundations of Success: A Harvard-Trained Scientist Separates the Science of Success from Self-Help Snake Oil* (San Francisco: Next Level Sciences, 2002), 110.

14. Oswald Chambers, *My Utmost for His Highest,* classic ed. (Grand Rapids, MI: Discovery House, 2017), August 3.

15. Numbers 14:34.

16. Psalm 84:10.

17. 2 Peter 3:8.

18. Pablo Casals, quoted in "I Feel That I Am Making Daily Progress," Quote Investigator, https://quoteinvestigator.com/2014/02 /12/casals-progress.

19. Eugene H. Peterson, *A Long Obedience in the Same Direction: Discipleship in an Instant Society,* commemorative ed. (Downers Grove, IL: IVP Books, 2019).

20. Galatians 6:9.

HABIT 7: SEED THE CLOUDS

1. Ginger Strand, *The Brothers Vonnegut: Science and Fiction in the House of Magic* (New York: Farrar, Straus, and Giroux, 2015), 58.

2. 1 Kings 18:42, NLT.

3. Howard Schulz, *Pour Your Heart into It: How Starbucks Built a Company One Cup at a Time* (New York: Hyperion, 1997), 63. This quote, to be exact, is referring to when Schultz decided to leave Starbucks in 1985 as their director of retail operations and marketing and start a company that brewed individual coffee and

espresso beverages, having been so inspired by the popularity of espresso bars in Milan, Italy. His company acquired Starbucks assets in 1987, and Schultz, along with Howard Behar and Orin Smith, went on to make Starbucks an international brand.

4. Schultz, *Pour Your Heart,* 185.

5. David Brooks, *On Paradise Drive: How We Live (and Always Have) in the Future Tense* (New York: Simon & Schuster, 2005), 263.

6. Brooks, *On Paradise Drive,* 263.

7. 1 Kings 18:43–44.

8. Hayim Nahman Bialik and Yehoshua Hana Ravnitzy, eds., *The Book of Legends—Sefer Ha-Aggadah: Legends from the Talmud and Midrash,* trans., William G. Braude (New York: Schocken, 1992), 202.

9. Wikipedia, s.v. "Jadav Payeng," last modified September 5, 2020, https://en.wikipedia.org/wiki/Jadav_Payeng.

10. William D McMaster, *Forest Man,* YouTube video, 16:34, www.youtube.com/watch?v=HkZDSqyE1do.

Chapter 13: Now or Never

1. Hermann Weyl, *Symmetry* (Princeton, NJ: Princeton University Press, 2016), 138.

2. Wikipedia, s.v. "Évariste Galois," last modified June 21, 2020, 21:27, https://en.wikipedia.org/wiki/%C3%89variste_Galois.

3. "Évariste Galois," Galois, https://galois.com/team/evariste-galois.

4. E. T. Bell, *Men of Mathematics: The Lives and Achievements of the Great Mathematicians from Zeno to Poincaré* (New York: Touchstone, 1986), 375.

5. Bell, *Men of Mathematics,* 375.

6. Shai Danziger, Jonathan Levav, and Liora Avnaim-Pesso, "Extraneous Factors in Judicial Decisions," *PNAS* 108, no. 17 (2011): 6889–92; Marshall Goldsmith, *Triggers: Creating Behavior That Lasts, Becoming the Person You Want to Be* (New York: Crown Business, 2015), 183.

7. John 18:10.

8. John 18:15–18, 25–27.

9. Mark 14:51–52.

10. Matthew 26:40–43.

11. Jonathan Levav, quoted in Binyamin Appelbaum, "Up for Parole? Better Hope You're First on the Docket," Economix, April 14, 2011, https://economix.blogs.nytimes.com/2011/04/14/time-and -judgment.

12. Ray Williams, "How Neuroscience Can Help Us Make Better Decisions," Ray Williams, https://raywilliams.ca/neuroscience -can-help-us-make-better-decisions.

13. John Donne, "From a Sermon Preached 12 December 1626," in *John Donne: The Major Works,* ed. John Carey (New York: Oxford University Press, 2000), 373.

14. Blaise Pascal, *Pensées,* trans. A. J. Krailsheimer, rev. ed. (London: Penguin Books, 1995), 37.

15. Philippians 4:8.

16. Luke 12:27, ESV.

17. Andrea Wulf, "*Walden* Wasn't Thoreau's Masterpiece," *Atlantic,* November 2017, www.theatlantic.com/magazine/archive/2017 /11/what-thoreau-saw/540615.

18. Laura Dassow Walls, quoted in Wulf, "*Walden* Wasn't Thoreau's Masterpiece."

19. Blaise Pascal, *Pensees* (New York: Penguin, 1995), 136.

20. Ecclesiastes 11:4.

21. Ecclesiastes 11:6.

22. Andy Stanley, *Next Generation Leader: Five Essentials for Those Who Will Shape the Future* (Colorado Springs: Multnomah, 2003), 93.

23. John D. Rockefeller, quoted in Christopher Klein, "10 Things You May Not Know About John D. Rockefeller," History.com, last modified September 1, 2018, www.history.com/news/10 -things-you-may-not-know-about-john-d-rockefeller.

24. Mark Stevens, *Rich Is a Religion: Breaking the Timeless Code to Wealth* (Hoboken, NJ: John Wiley & Sons, 2008), 135.

25. "John D. Rockefeller Net Worth," Celebrity Net Worth, www .celebritynetworth.com/richest-businessmen/richest-billionaires /john-rockefeller-net-worth.

26. Ron Chernow, *Titan: The Life of John D. Rockefeller, Sr.,* 2nd ed. (New York: Vintage Books, 2004), 45–46.

27. Romans 14:5.

28. Exodus 12:17–18, AMPC.

29. Wikipedia, s.v. "Jewish Holidays," last modified July 31, 2020, 23:34, https://en.wikipedia.org/wiki/Jewish_holidays.

30. Numbers 10:10.
31. *Meet the Parents,* directed by Jay Roach (Universal City, CA: Universal Pictures, 2000).
32. Nehemiah 9:19, TLB.
33. Psalm 110:3, TLB.
34. 2 Corinthians 4:16.
35. Luke 11:3, KJV.

EPILOGUE: THE GAME WITH MINUTES

1. 1 Samuel 17:54, ESV.
2. Ephesians 2:10.
3. Joshua 6:2.
4. Thomas Shepard, quoted in Alexander Whyte, *Thomas Shepard: Pilgrim Father and Founder of Harvard* (Edinburgh: O. Anderson and Ferrier, 1909), 34.
5. Shepard, quoted in Whyte, *Thomas Shepard,* 34.
6. Frank Charles Laubach, *The Game with Minutes* (Eastford, CT: Martino Fine, 2012), 47.
7. Frank C. Laubach, *Letters by a Modern Mystic* (London: Society for Promoting Christian Knowledge, 2011), 39.
8. Laubach, *The Game with Minutes,* 44.
9. Laubach, *The Game with Minutes,* 47.
10. Laubach, *The Game with Minutes,* 46.
11. Psalm 118:24, ESV.
12. Matthew 6:11, ESV.
13. Lamentations 3:22–23, ESV.
14. Psalm 23:6, ESV.

About the Author

Mark Batterson is the lead pastor of National Community Church (National.CC) in Washington, DC. One church in seven locations, NCC owns and operates Ebenezers Coffeehouse, the Miracle Theatre, and the DC Dream Center. NCC is currently developing a city block into the Capital Turnaround. This 100,000-square-foot space will include an event venue, child development center, mixed-use marketplace, and coworking space.

Mark holds a doctor of ministry degree from Regent University and is the *New York Times* bestselling author of twenty books, including *The Circle Maker, Chase the Lion, In a Pit with a Lion on a Snowy Day,* and *Whisper.* He and his wife, Lora, have three children and live on Capitol Hill.

You can follow Mark @markbatterson on Twitter, Instagram, and Facebook.

You can find Mark online at www.markbatterson.com.

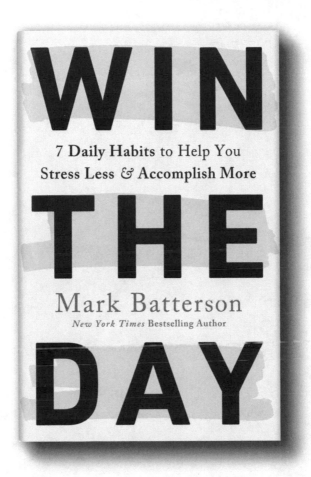

Free Resources Available at
markbatterson.com/wintheday

- Sermon Series Video, Graphics, and Downloads
- Small Group Discussion Guide
- Steps to Setting Life Goals
- Life Goal List
- And More!

MULTNOMAH

waterbrookmultnomah.com

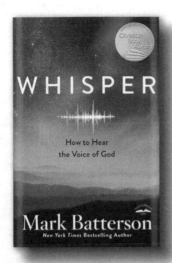

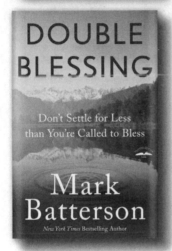

Start reading your next
MARK BATTERSON
book today!

WIN
THE
DAY

by Mark Batterson

Follow Mark!

@markbatterson

7 HABITS

1. Flip the Script

2. Kiss the Wave

3. Eat the Frog

4. Fly the Kite

5. Cut the Rope

6. Wind the Clock

7. Seed the Clouds

#WINTHEDAY